LEIBNIZ'S NEW ESSAYS CONCERNING THE HUMAN UNDERSTANDING.

LEIBNIZ'S

NEW ESSAYS CONCERNING THE HUMAN UNDERSTANDING.

A CRITICAL EXPOSITION.

BY

JOHN DEWEY PH.D.,

ASSISTANT PROFESSOR OF PHILOSOPHY IN THE UNIVERSITY OF

MICHIGAN, AND PROFESSOR (KLECT) OF MENTAL AND

MORAL PHILOSOPHY IN THE UNIVERSITY
OF MINXESOTA

ISBN: 978-93-5128-977-7(HB)

First Published in 1888
Indian Reprint in 2017

Published by

Kalpaz Publications
C-30, Satyawati Nagar,
Delhi – 110052
E-mail: kalpaz@hotmail.com
Website: kalpazpublications.com
Ph.: +91-9212142040

Cataloging in Publication Data—DK
Courtesy: D.K. Agencies (P) Ltd. <docinfo@dkagencies.com>

Dewey, John, 1859-1952, **author.**
Leibniz's new essays concerning the human understanding : a critical exposition / by John Dewey (Ph.D.).
pages cm
"First published in 1888"—Title page verso.
ISBN 9789351289777 (HB)

1. Leibniz, Gottfried Wilhelm, Freiherr von, 1646-1716. Nouveaux essais sur l'entendement humain. 2. Knowledge, Theory of. I. Title.

B2581.Z7D49 2017 DDC 121 23

PREFACE.

THE purpose of the series of which the present volume is one, is not, as will be seen by reference to the statement in the initial volume, to sum up *in toto* the system of any philosopher, but to give a "critical exposition" of some one masterpiece. In treating the "Nouveaux Essais" of Leibniz, I have found myself obliged, at times, to violate the letter of this expressed intention, in order to fulfil its spirit. The "Nouveaux Essais," in spite of its being one of the two most extended philosophical writings of Leibniz, is a compendium of comments, rather than a connected argument or exposition. It has all the suggestiveness and richness of a note-book, but with much also of its fragmentariness. I have therefore been obliged to supplement my account of it by constant references to the other writings of Leibniz, and occasionally to take considerable liberty with the order of the treatment of topics. Upon the whole, this book will be found, I hope, to be a faithful reflex not only of Leibniz's thought, but also of his discussions in the "Nouveaux Essais."

In the main, the course of philosophic thought since the time of Leibniz has been such as to render almost self-evident his limitations, and to suggest needed corrections and amplifications. Indeed, it is much easier for those whose thoughts follow the turn that Kant has given modern thinking to appreciate the defects of Leibniz than to realize his greatness. I have endeavored, therefore, in the body of the work, to identify my thought with that of Leibniz as much as possible, to assume his standpoint and method, and, for the most part, to confine express criticism upon his limitations to the final chapter. In particular, I have attempted to bring out the relations of philosophy to the growing science of his times, to state the doctrine of pre-established harmony as he himself meant it, and to give something like consistency and coherency to his doctrine of material existence and of nature. This last task seemed especially to require doing. I have also endeavored to keep in mind, throughout, Leibniz's relations to Locke, and to show the "Nouveaux Essais" as typical of the distinction between characteristic British and German thought.

JOHN DEWEY.

May, 1888.

CONTENTS.

CHAPTER I.

The Man.

CHAPTER II.

Sources of his Philosophy.

CHAPTER III.

The Problem and its Solution.

CHAPTER IV.

Locke and Leibniz. — Innate Ideas.

CHAPTER V.

Sensation and Experience.

CHAPTER VI.

The Impulses and the Will.

CHAPTER VII.

MATTER AND ITS RELATION TO SPIRIT.

CHAPTER VIII.

MATERIAL PHENOMENA AND THEIR REALITY.

CHAPTER IX.

SOME FUNDAMENTAL CONCEPTIONS.

CHAPTER X.

The Nature and Extent of Knowledge.

CHAPTER XI.

THE THEOLOGY OF LEIBNIZ.

CHAPTER XII.

Criticism and Conclusion.

LEIBNIZ'S NEW ESSAYS

CONCERNING

THE HUMAN UNDERSTANDING.

CHAPTER I.

THE MAN.

"HE who knows me only by my writings does not know me," said Leibniz. These words — true, indeed, of every writer, but true of Leibniz in a way which gives a peculiar interest and charm to his life — must be our excuse for prefacing what is to be said of his "New Essays concerning the Human Understanding" with a brief biographical sketch.

Gottfried Wilhelm Leibniz was born in Leipzig June 21, 1646. His father, who died when Leibniz was only six years old, was a professor in the university and a notary of considerable practice. From him the future philosopher seems to have derived his extraordinary industry and love of detail. Such accounts as we have of him show no traces of the wonderful intellectual genius of his son, but only a diligent, plodding, faithful, and religious man, a thoroughly conscientious husband, jurist, and professor. Nor in the lines of physical heredity can we account for the unique career of Leibniz by his mother's endowments. The fact, however, that she was patient in all trial, living in peace with her neighbors, anxious for unity and concord with all people, even with those not well disposed to her, throws great light upon the fundamental trait of Leibniz's ethical nature. As in so many cases, it is the inherited moral characteristics which form the basis of the intellectual nature. The love of unity which was a moral trait in Leibniz's mother became in him the hunger for a harmonious and unified mental world; the father's devotion to detail showed itself as the desire for knowledge as minute and comprehensive as it was inter-related.

Left without his father, he was by the advice of a discerning friend allowed free access to the library. Leibniz never ceased to count this one of the greatest fortunes of his life. Writing in after years to a friend, he says: —

"When I lost my father, and was left without any direction in my studies, I had the luck to get at books in all languages, of all religions, upon all sciences, and to read them without any regular order, just as my own impulse led me. From this I obtained the great advantage that I was freed from ordinary prejudices, and introduced to many things of which I should otherwise never have thought."

In a philosophical essay, in which he describes himself under the name of Gulielmus Pacidius, he says: —

"Wilhelm Friedlieb, a German by birth, who lost his father in his early years, was led to study through the innate tendency of his spirit; and the freedom with which he moved about in the sciences was equal to this innate impulse. He buried himself, a boy eight years old, in a library, staying there sometimes whole days, and, hardly stammering Latin, he took up every book which pleased his eyes. Opening and shutting them without any choice, he sipped now here, now there, lost himself in one, skipped over another, as the clearness of expression or of content attracted him. He seemed to be directed by the *Tolle et lege* of a higher voice. As good fortune would have it, he gave himself up to the ancients, in whom he at first understood nothing, by degrees a little, finally all that was really necessary, until he assumed not only a certain coloring of their expression, but also of their thought, — just as those who go about in the sun, even while they are occupied with other things, get sun-browned."

And he goes on to tell us that their influence always remained with him. Their human, their important, their comprehensive ideas, grasping the whole of life in one image, together with their clear, natural, and transparent mode of expression, adapted precisely to their thoughts, seemed to him to be in the greatest contrast with the writings of moderns, without definiteness or order in expression, and without vitality or purpose in thought, — "written as if for another world." Thus Leibniz learned two of the great lessons of his life,—to seek always for clearness of diction and for pertinence and purpose of ideas.

Historians and poets first occupied him; but when in his school-life, a lad of twelve or thirteen years, he came to the study of logic, he was greatly struck, he says, by the "ordering and analysis of thoughts which he found there." He gave himself up to making tables of categories and predicaments, analyzing each book that he read into suitable topics, and arranging these into classes and sub-classes. We can imagine the astonishment of his playmates as he burst upon them with a demand to classify this or that idea, to find its appropriate predicament. Thus he was led naturally to the philosophic books in his father's library,—to Plato and to Aristotle, to the Scholastics. Suarez, in particular, among the latter, he read; and traces of his influences are to be found in the formulation of his own philosophic system. At about this same time he took great delight in the theological works with which his father's library abounded, reading with equal ease and pleasure the writings of the Lutherans and of the Reformed Church, of the Jesuits and the Jansenists, of the Thomists and the Arminians. The result was, he tells us, that he was strengthened in the Lutheran faith of his family, but, as we may easily imagine from his after life, made tolerant of all forms of faith.

In 1661 the boy Leibniz, fifteen years old, entered the University of Leipzig. If we glance back upon his attainments, we find him thoroughly at home in Latin, having made good progress in Greek, acquainted with the historians and poets of antiquity, acquainted with the contemporary range of science, except in mathematics and physics, deeply read and interested in ancient and scholastic philosophy and in the current theological discussions. Of himself he says: —

"Two things were of extraordinary aid to me: in the first place, I was self-taught; and in the second, as soon as I entered upon any science I sought for something new, even though I did not as yet thoroughly understand the old. I thus gained two things: I did not fill my mind with things empty and to be unlearned afterwards, — things resting upon the assertion of the teacher, and not upon reason; and secondly, I never rested till I got down to the very roots of the science and reached its principles."

While there is always a temptation to force the facts which we know of a man's early life, so as to make them seem to account for what appears in mature years, and to find symbolisms and analogies which do not exist, we are not going astray, I think, if we see foreshadowed in this early education of Leibniz the two leading traits of his later thought, — universality and individuality. The range of Leibniz's investigations already marks him as one who will be content with no fundamental principle which does not mirror the universe. The freedom with which he carried them on is testimony to the fact that even at this age the idea of self-development, of individual growth from within, was working upon him. In the fact, also, that he was self-taught we find doubtless the reason that he alone of the thinkers of this period did not have to retrace his steps, to take a hostile attitude towards the ideas into which he was educated, and to start anew upon a foundation then first built. The development of the thought of Leibniz is so gradual, continuous, and constant that it may serve as a model of the law by which the "monad" acts. Is not his early acquaintance with ancient literature and mediæval philosophy the reason that he could afterwards write that his philosophical system "connects Plato with Democritus, Aristotle with Descartes, the Scholastics with the moderns, theology and morals with reason"? And who can fail to see in the impartiality, the comprehensiveness, of his self-education the prophecy of the time when he can write of his ideas that "there are united in them, as in a centre of perspective, the ideas of the Sceptics in attributing to sensible things only a slight degree of reality; of the Pythagoreans and Platonists, who reduce all to harmonies, numbers, and ideas; of Parmenides and Plotinus, with their One and All; of the Stoics, with their notion of necessity, compatible with the spontaneity of other schools; of the vital philosophy of the Cabalists, who find feeling everywhere; of the forms and entelechies of Aristotle and the Schoolmen, united with the mechanical explanation of phenomena according to Democritus and the moderns"?

But we must hurry along over the succeeding years of his life. In the university the study of law was his principal occupation, as he had decided to follow in the footsteps of his father. It cannot be said that the character of the instruction or of the instructors at Leipzig was such as to give much nutriment or stimulus to a mind like that of Leibniz. He became acquainted there, however, with the Italian philosophy of the sixteenth century, — a philosophy which, as formulated by Cardanus and Campanella, formed the transition from Scholastic philosophy to the "mechanical" mode of viewing the universe. He had here also his first introduction to Descartes. The consequences of the new vision opened to Leibniz must be told in his own words: "I was but a child when I came to know Aristotle; even the Scholastics did not frighten me; and I in no way regret this now. Plato and Plotinus gave me much delight, not to speak of other philosophers of antiquity. Then I fell in with the writings of modern philosophy, and I recall the time when, a boy of fifteen years, I went walking in a little wood near Leipzig, the Rosenthal, in order to consider whether I should hold to the doctrine of substantial forms. Finally the mechanical theory conquered, and thus I was led to the study of the mathematical sciences."

To the study of the mathematical sciences! Surely words of no mean import for either the future of Leibniz or of mathematics. But his Leipzig studies did not take him very far in this new direction. Only the elements of Euclid were taught there, and these by a lecturer of such confused style that Leibniz seems alone to have understood them. In Jena, however, where he went for a semester, things were somewhat better. Weigel, a mathematician of some fame, an astronomer, a jurist, and a philosopher, taught there, and introduced Leibniz into the lower forms of analysis. But the Thirty Years' War had not left Germany in a state of high culture, and in after years Leibniz lamented the limitations of his early mathematical training, remarking that if he had spent his youth in Paris, he would have enriched science earlier. By 1666 Leibniz had finished his university career, having in previous years attained the degrees of bachelor of philosophy and master of philosophy. It is significant that for the first he wrote a thesis upon the principle of individuation, — the principle which in later years became the basis of his philosophy. This early essay, however, is rather an exhibition of learning and of dexterity in handling logical methods than a real anticipation of his after-thought.

For his second degree, he wrote a thesis upon the application of philosophic ideas to juridic procedure, — considerations which never ceased to occupy him. At about the same time appeared his earliest independent work, "De Arte Combinatoria." From his study of mathematics, and especially of algebraic methods, Leibniz had become convinced that the source of all science is, — first, analysis; second, symbolic representation of the fundamental concepts, the symbolism avoiding the ambiguities and vagueness of language; and thirdly, the synthesis and interpretation of the symbols. It seemed to Leibniz that it ought to be possible to find the simplest notions in all the sciences, to discover general rules for calculating all their varieties of combination, and thus to attain the same certainty and generality of result that characterize mathematics. Leibniz never gave up this thought. Indeed, in spirit his philosophy is but its application, with the omission of symbols, on the side of the general notions fundamental to all science. It was also the idea of his age, — the idea that inspired Spinoza and the *Aufklärung*, the idea that inspired philosophical thinking until Kant gave it its death-blow by demonstrating the distinction between the methods of philosophy and of mathematical and physical science.

In 1666 Leibniz should have received his double doctorate of philosophy and of law; but petty jealousies and personal fears prevented his presenting himself for the examination. Disgusted with his treatment, feeling that the ties that bound him to Leipzig were severed by the recent death of his mother, anxious to study mathematics further, and, as he confesses, desiring, with the natural eagerness of youth, to see more of the world, he left Leipzig forever, and entered upon his *Wanderjahre*. He was prepared to be no mean citizen of the world. In his education he had gone from the historians to the poets, from the poets to the philosophers and the Scholastics, from them to the theologians and Church Fathers, then to the jurists, to the mathematicians, and then again to philosophy and to law.

He first directed his steps to the University of Altdorf; here he obtained his doctorate in law, and was offered a professorship, which he declined,—apparently because he felt that his time was not yet come, and that when it should come, it would not be in the narrow limits of a country village. From Altdorf he went to Nürnberg; here all that need concern us is the fact that he joined a society of alchemists (*fraternitas roseæcrucis*), and was made their secretary. Hereby he gained three things,—a knowledge of chemistry; an acquaintance with a number of scientific men of different countries, with whom, as secretary, he carried on correspondence; and the friendship of Boineburg, a diplomat of the court of the Elector and Archbishop of Mainz. This friendship was the means of his removing to Frankfurt. Here, under the direction of the Elector, he engaged in remodelling Roman law so as to adapt it for German use, in writing diplomatic tracts, letters, and essays upon theological matters, and in editing an edition of Nizolius,—a now forgotten philosophical writer. One of the most noteworthy facts in connection with this edition is that Leibniz pointed out the fitness of the German language for philosophical uses, and urged its employment,—a memorable fact in connection with the later development of German thought. Another important tract which he wrote was one urging the alliance of all the German States for the purpose of advancing their internal and common interests. Here, as so often, Leibniz was almost two centuries in advance of his times. But the chief thing in connection with the stay of Leibniz at Mainz was the cause for which he left it. Louis XIV. had broken up the Triple Alliance, and showed signs of attacking Holland and the German Empire. It was then proposed to him that it would be of greater glory to himself and of greater advantage to France that he should move against Turkey and Egypt. The mission of presenting these ideas to the great king was intrusted to Leibniz, and in 1672 he went to Paris.

The plan failed completely, — so completely that we need say no more about it. But the journey to Paris was none the less the turning-point in the career of Leibniz. It brought him to the centre of intellectual civilization, — to a centre compared with which the highest attainments of disrupted and disheartened Germany were comparative barbarism. Molière was still alive, and Racine was at the summit of his glory. Leibniz became acquainted with Arnaud, a disciple of Descartes, who initiated him into the motive and spirit of his master. Cartesianism as a system, with its scientific basis and its speculative consequences, thus first became to him an intellectual reality. And, perhaps most important of all, he met Huygens, who became his teacher and inspirer both in the higher forms of mathematics and in their application to the interpretation and expression of physical phenomena. His diplomatic mission took him also to London, where the growing world of mathematical science was opened yet wider to him. The name of Sir Isaac Newton need only be given to show what this meant. From this time one of the greatest glories of Leibniz's life dates, — a glory, however, which during his lifetime was embittered by envy and unappreciation, and obscured by detraction and malice, — the invention of the infinitesimal calculus. It would be interesting, were this the place, to trace the history of its discovery, — the gradual steps which led to it, the physical facts as well as mathematical theories which made it a necessity; but it must suffice to mention that these were such that the discovery of some general mode of expressing and interpreting the newly discovered facts of Nature was absolutely required for the further advance of science, and that steps towards the introduction of the fundamental ideas of the calculus had already been taken, — notably by Keppler, by Cavalieri, and by Wallis. It would be interesting to follow also the course of the controversy with Newton, — a controversy which in its method of conduct reflects no credit upon the names of either. But this can be summed up by saying that it is now generally admitted that absolute priority belongs to Newton, but that entire independence and originality characterize none the less the work of Leibniz, and that the method of approach and statement of the latter are the more philosophical and general, and, to use the words of the judicious summary of Merz, "Newton cared more for the results than the principle, while Leibniz was in search of fundamental principles, and anxious to arrive at simplifications and generalizations."

The death of Boineburg removed the especial reasons for the return of Leibniz to Frankfurt, and in 1676 he accepted the position of librarian and private councillor at the court of Hanover. It arouses our interest and our questionings to know that on his journey back he stopped at the Hague, and there met face to face the other future great philosopher of the time, Spinoza. But our questionings meet no answer. At Hanover, the industries of Leibniz were varied. An extract from one of his own letters, though written at a somewhat later date, will give the best outline of his activities.

"It is incredible how scattered and divided are my occupations. I burrow through archives, investigate old writings, and collect unprinted manuscripts, with a view to throwing light on the history of Brunswick. I also receive and write a countless number of letters. I have so much that is new in mathematics, so many thoughts in philosophy, so many literary observations which I cannot get into shape, that in the midst of my tasks I do not know where to begin, and with Ovid am inclined to cry out: 'My riches make me poor.' I should like to give a description of my calculating-machine; but time fails. Above all else I desire to complete my

Dynamics, as I think that I have finally discovered the true laws of material Nature, by whose means problems about bodies which are out of reach of rules now known may be solved. Friends are urging me to publish my Science of the Infinite, containing the basis of my new analysis. I have also on hand a new Characteristic, and many general considerations about the art of discovery. But all these works, the historical excepted, have to be done at odd moments. Then at the court all sorts of things are expected. I have to answer questions on points in international law; on points concerning the rights of the various princes in the Empire: so far I have managed to keep out of questions of private law. With all this I have had to carry on negotiations with the bishops of Neustadt and of Meaux [Bossuet], and with Pelisson and others upon religious matters."

It is interesting to note how the philosophic spirit, the instinct for unity and generality, showed itself even in the least of Leibniz's tasks. The Duke of Brunswick imposed upon Leibniz the task of drawing up a genealogical table of his House. Under Leibniz's hands this expanded into a history of the House, and this in turn was the centre of an important study of the German Empire. It was impossible that the philosopher, according to whom every real being reflected the whole of the universe from its point of view, should have been able to treat even a slight phase of local history without regarding it in its relations to the history of the world. Similarly some mining operations in the Harz Mountains called the attention of Leibniz to geological matters. The result was a treatise called "Protogäa," in which Leibniz gave a history of the development of the earth. Not content with seeing in a Brunswick mountain an epitome of the world's physical formation, it was his intention to make this an introduction to his political history as a sort of geographical background and foundation. It is interesting to note that the historical studies of Leibniz took him on a three years' journey, from 1687 to 1690, through the various courts of Europe, — a fact which not only had considerable influence upon Leibniz himself, but which enabled him to give stimulus to scientific development in more ways and places than one.

His philosophical career as an author begins for the most part with his return to Hanover in 1690. This lies outside of the scope of the present chapter, but here is a convenient place to call attention to the fact that for Leibniz the multitude of his other duties was so great that his philosophical work was the work "of odd moments." There is no systematic exposition; there are a vast number of letters, of essays, of abstracts and memoranda published in various scientific journals. His philosophy bears not only in form, but in substance, traces of its haphazard and desultory origin. Another point of interest in this connection is the degree to which, in form, at least, his philosophical writings bear the impress of his cosmopolitan life. Leibniz had seen too much of the world, too much of courts, for his thoughts to take the rigid and unbending form of geometrical exposition suited to the lonely student of the Hague. Nor was the regular progression and elucidation of ideas adapted to the later Germans, almost without exception university professors, suited to the man of affairs. There is everywhere in Leibniz the attempt to adapt his modes of statement, not only to the terminology, but even to the ideas, of the one to whom they are addressed. There is the desire to magnify points of agreement, to minimize disagreements, characteristic of the courtier and the diplomat. His comprehensiveness is not only a comprehensiveness of thought, but of ways of exposition, due very largely, we must think, to his cosmopolitan education. The result has been to the great detriment of Leibniz's influence as a systematic thinker, although it may be argued that it has aided his indirect and suggestive influence, the absorption of his ideas by men of literature, by Goethe, above all by Lessing, and his stimulating effect upon science and philosophy. It is certain that the attempt to systematize his thoughts, as was done by Wolff, had for its result the disappearance of all that was profound and thought-exciting.

If his philosophy thus reflects the manner of his daily life, the occupations of the latter were informed by the spirit of his philosophy. Two of the dearest interests of Leibniz remain to be mentioned, — one, the founding of academies ; the other, the reconciling of religious organizations. The former testifies to his desire for comprehensiveness, unity, and organization of knowledge; the latter to his desire for practical unity, his dislike of all that is opposed and isolated. His efforts in the religious direction were twofold. The first was to end the theological and political controversies of the time by the reunion of the Protestant and Roman Catholic Churches. It was a plan which did the greatest honor to the pacific spirit of Leibniz, but it was predestined to failure. Both sides made concessions, — more concessions than we of to-day should believe possible. But the one thing the Roman Catholic Church would not concede was the one thing which the Protestant Church demanded, — the notion of authority and hierarchy. Indeed, it may be questioned whether the terms on which Leibniz conceived of their reunion do not point to the greatest weakness in his philosophy, — the tendency to overlook oppositions and to resolve all contradiction into differences of degree. Hardly had this plan fallen through when Leibniz turned to the project of a union of the Lutheran and Reformed branches of the Protestant Church. This scheme was more hopeful, and while unrealized during the life of our philosopher, was afterwards accomplished.

It is noteworthy that even before Leibniz went to Paris and to London he had conceived the idea of a society of learned men for the investigation, the systematization, and the publication of scientific truth in all its varied forms, — a society which should in breadth include the whole sphere of sciences, but should not treat them as so many isolated disciplines, but as members of one system. This idea was quickened when Leibniz saw the degree in which it had already been realized in the two great world-capitals. He never ceased to try to introduce similar academies wherever he had influence. In 1700 his labors bore their fruit in one instance. The Academy at Berlin was founded, and Leibniz was its first, and indeed life-long, president. But disappointment met him at Vienna, Dresden, and St. Petersburg, where he proposed similar societies.

Any sketch of Leibniz's life, however brief, would be imperfect which did not mention the names at least of two remarkable women, — remarkable in themselves, and remarkable in their friendship with Leibniz. These were Sophia, grand-daughter of James I. of England (and thus the link by which the House of Brunswick finally came to rule over Great Britain) and wife of the Duke of Brunswick, and her daughter Sophia Charlotte, wife of the first king of Prussia. The latter, in particular, gave Leibniz every encouragement. She was personally deeply interested in all theological and philosophical questions. Upon her death-bed, in 1705, she is said to have told those about her that they were not to mourn for her, as she should now be able to satisfy her desire to learn about things which Leibniz had never sufficiently explained.

Her death marks the beginning of a period in

Leibniz's life which it is not pleasant to dwell upon. New rulers arose that knew not Leibniz. It cannot be said that from this time till his death in Hanover in 1716 Leibniz had much joy or satisfaction. His best friends were dead; his political ambitions were disappointed; he was suspected of coldness and unfriendliness by the courts both of Berlin and Hanover; Paris and Vienna were closed to him, so far as any wide influence was concerned, by his religious faith; the controversy with the friends of Newton still followed him. He was a man of the most remarkable intellectual gifts, of an energy which could be satisfied only with wide fields of action; and he found himself shut in by narrow intrigue to a petty round of courtly officialism. It is little wonder that the following words fell from his lips: "Germany is the only country in the world that does not know how to recognize the fame of its children and to make that fame immortal. It forgets itself; it forgets its own, unless foreigners make it mindful of its own treasures." A Scotch friend of Leibniz, who happened to be in Hanover when he died, wrote that Leibniz "was buried more like a robber than what he really was, — the ornament of his country." Such was the mortal end of the greatest intellectual genius since Aristotle. But genius is not a matter to be bounded in life or in death by provincial courts. Leibniz remains a foremost citizen in that "Kingdom of Spirits" in whose formation he found the meaning of the world.

CHAPTER II.

THE SOURCES OF HIS PHILOSOPHY.

WHAT is true of all men is true of philosophers, and of Leibniz among them. Speaking generally, what they are unconsciously and fundamentally, they are through absorption of their antecedents and surroundings. What they are consciously and reflectively, they are through their reaction upon the influence of heredity and environment. But there is a spiritual line of descent and a spiritual atmosphere; and in speaking of a philosopher, it is with this intellectual heredity and environment, rather than with the physical, that we are concerned. Leibniz was born into a period of intellectual activity the most teeming with ideas, the most fruitful in results, of any, perhaps, since the age of Pericles. We pride ourselves justly upon the activity of our own century, and in diffusion of intellectual action and wide-spread application of ideas the age of Leibniz could not compare with it. But ours *is* the age of diffusion and application, while his was one of fermentation and birth.

Such a period in its earlier days is apt to be turbid and unsettled. There is more heat of friction than calm light. And such had been the case in the hundred years before Leibniz. But when he arrived at intellectual maturity much of the crudity had disappeared. The troubling of the waters of thought had ceased; they were becoming clarified. Bacon, Hobbes, Descartes, each had crystallized something out of that seething and chaotic mass of new ideas which had forced itself into European consciousness. Men had been introduced into a new world, and the natural result had been feelings of strangeness, and the vagaries of intellectual wanderings. But by the day of Leibniz the intellectual bearings had been made out anew, the new mental orientation had been secured.

The marks of this "new spiritual picture of the universe" are everywhere to be seen in Leibniz. His philosophy is the dawning consciousness of the modern world. In it we see the very conception and birth of the modern interpretation of the world. The history of thought is one continuous testimony to the ease with which we become hardened to ideas through custom. Ideas are constantly precipitating themselves out of the realm of ideas into that of ways of thinking and of viewing the universe. The problem of one century is the axiom of another. What one generation stakes its activity upon investigating is quietly taken for granted by the next. And so the highest reach of intellectual inspiration in the sixteenth century is to-day the ordinary food of thought, accepted without an inquiry as to its source, and almost without a suspicion that it has a recent historic origin. We have to go to Bacon or to Leibniz to see the genesis and growth of those ideas which to-day have become materialized into axiomatic points of view and into hard-and-fast categories of thought. In reading Leibniz the idea comes over us in all its freshness that there was a time when it was a discovery that the world is a universe, made after one plan and of one stuff. The ideas of inter-relation, of the harmony of law, of mutual dependence and correspondence, were not always the assumed starting-points of thought; they were once the crowning discoveries of a philosophy aglow and almost intoxicated with the splendor of its far-reaching generalizations. I take these examples of the unity of the world, the continuity and interdependence of all within it, because these are the ideas which come to their conscious and delighted birth in the philosophy of Leibniz. We do not put ourselves into the right attitude for understanding his thought until we remember that these ideas — the commonest tools of our thinking — were once new and fresh, and in their novelty and transforming strangeness were the products of a philosophic interpretation of experience. Except in that later contemporary of Leibniz, the young and enthusiastic Irish idealist, Berkeley, I know of no historic thinker in whom the birth-throes (joyous, however) of a new conception of the world are so evident as in Leibniz. But while in Berkeley what we see is the young man carried away and astounded by the grandeur and simplicity of a "new way of ideas" which he has discovered, what we see in Leibniz is the mature man penetrated throughout his being with an idea which in its unity answers to the unity of the world, and which in its complexity answers, tone to tone, to the complex harmony of the world.

The familiarity of the ideas which we use hides their grandeur from us. The unity of the world is a matter of course with us; the dependent order of all within it a mere starting-point upon which to base our investigations. But if we will put ourselves in the position of Leibniz, and behold, not the new planet, but the new universe, so one, so linked together, swimming into our ken, we shall feel something of the same exultant thrill that Leibniz felt,—an exultation not indeed personal in its nature, but which arises from the expansion of the human mind face to face with an expanding world. The spirit which is at the heart of the philosophy of Leibniz is the spirit which speaks in the following words: "Quin imo qui unam partem materiæ comprehenderet, idem comprehenderet totum universum ob eandem περιχώρησιν quam dixi. Mea principia talia sunt, ut vix a se invicem develli possint. Qui unum bene novit, omnia novit." It is a spirit which feels that the secret of the universe has been rendered up to it, and which breathes a buoyant optimism. And if we of the nineteenth century have chosen to bewail the complexity of the problem of life, and to run hither and thither multiplying "insights" and points of view till this enthusiastic confidence in reason seems to us the rashness of an ignorance which does not comprehend the problem, and the unity in which Leibniz rested appears cold and abstract beside the manifold richness of the world, we should not forget that after all we have incorporated into our very mental structure the fundamental thoughts of Leibniz,— the thoughts of the rationality of the universe and of the "reign of law."

What was the origin of these ideas in the mind of Leibniz? What influences in the philosophic succession of thinkers led him in this direction? What agencies acting in the intellectual world about him shaped his ideal reproduction of reality? Two causes above all others stand out with prominence, — one, the discoveries and principles of modern physical science; the other, that interpretation of experience which centuries before had been formulated by Aristotle. Leibniz has a double interest for those of to-day who reverence science and who hold to the historical method. His philosophy was an attempt to set in order the methods and principles of that growing science of nature which even then was transforming the emotional and mental life of Europe; and the attempt was guided everywhere by a profound and wide-reaching knowledge of the history of philosophy. On the first point Leibniz was certainly not alone. Bacon, Hobbes, Descartes, Spinoza, each felt in his own way the fructifying touch of the new-springing science, and had attempted under its guidance to interpret the facts of nature and of man. But Leibniz stood alone in his interest in the history of thought. He stands alone indeed till he is greeted by his compeers of the nineteenth century. To Bacon previous philosophy — the Greek, the scholastic — was an "eidol of the theatre." The human mind must be freed from its benumbing influence. To Descartes it was useless rubbish to be cleared away, that we might get a *tabula rasa* upon which to make a fresh start. And shall Locke and the empirical English school, or Reid and the Scotch school, or even Kant, be the first to throw a stone at Bacon and Descartes? It was reserved to Leibniz, with a genius almost two centuries in advance of his times, to penetrate the meaning of the previous development of reflective thought. It would be going beyond our brief to claim that Leibniz was interested in this *as* a historical movement, or that he specially concerned himself with the genetic lines which connected the various schools of thought. But we should come short of our duty to Leibniz if we did not recognize his conscious and largely successful attempt to apprehend the core of truth in all systems, however alien to his own, and to incorporate it into his own thinking.

Nothing could be more characteristic of Leibniz than his saying, "I find that most systems are right in a good share of that which they advance, but not so much in what they deny;" or than this other statement of his, "We must not hastily believe that which the mass of men, or even of authorities, advance, but each must demand for himself the proofs of the thesis sustained. Yet long research generally convinces that the old and received opinions are good, provided they be interpreted justly." It is in the profound union in Leibniz of the principles which these quotations image that his abiding worth lies. Leibniz was interested in affirmations, not in denials. He was interested in securing the union of the modern *method*, the spirit of original research and independent judgment, with the conserved *results* of previous thought. Leibniz was a man of his times; that is to say, he was a scientific man, — the contemporary, for example, of men as different as Bernouilli, Swammerdam, Huygens, and Newton, and was himself actively engaged in the prosecution of mathematics, mechanics, geology, comparative philology, and jurisprudence. But he was also a man of Aristotle's times, — that is to say, a philosopher, not satisfied until the facts, principles, and methods of science had received an interpretation which should explain and unify them.

Leibniz's acquaintance with the higher forms of mathematics was due, as we have seen, to his acquaintance with Huygens. As he made the acquaintance of the latter at the same time that he made the acquaintance of the followers of Descartes, it is likely that he received his introduction to the higher developments of the scientific interpretation of nature and of the philosophic interpretation of science at about the same time. For a while, then, Leibniz was a Cartesian; and he never ceased to call the doctrine of Descartes the antechamber of truth. What were the ideas which he received from Descartes? Fundamentally they were two, — one about the method of truth, the other about the substance of truth. He received the idea that the method of philosophy consists in the analysis of any complex group of ideas down to simple ideas which shall be perfectly clear and distinct; that all such clear and distinct ideas are true, and may then be used for the synthetic reconstruction of any body of truth. Concerning the substance of philosophic truth, he learned that nature is to be interpreted mechanically, and that the instrument of this mechanical interpretation is mathematics. I have used the term "received" in speaking of the relation of Leibniz to these ideas. Yet long before this time we might see him giving himself up to dreams about a vast art of combination which should reduce all the ideas concerned in any science to their simplest elements, and then combine them to any degree of complexity. We have already seen him giving us a picture of a boy of fifteen gravely disputing with himself whether he shall accept the doctrine of forms and final causes, or of physical causes, and as gravely deciding that he shall side with the "moderns;" and that boy was himself. In these facts we have renewed confirmation of the truth that one mind never receives from another anything excepting the stimulus, the reflex, the development of ideas which have already possessed it. But when Leibniz, with his isolated and somewhat ill-digested thoughts, came in contact with that systematized and connected body of doctrines which the Cartesians presented to him in Paris, his ideas were quickened, and he felt the necessity — that final mark of the philosophic mind — of putting them in order.

About the method of Descartes, which Leibniz adopted from him, or rather formulated for himself under the influence of Descartes, not much need be said. It was the method of Continental thought till the time of Kant. It was the mother of the philosophic systems of Descartes, Leibniz, and Spinoza. It was equally the mother of the German *Aufklärung* and the French *éclaircissement*. Its fundamental idea is the thought upon which Rationalism everywhere bases itself. It says: Reduce everything to simple notions. Get clearness; get distinctness. Analyze the complex. Shun the obscure. Discover axioms; employ these axioms in connection with the simple notions, and build up from them. Whatever can be treated in this way is capable of proof, and only this. Leibniz, I repeat, possessed this method in common with Descartes and Spinoza. The certainty and demonstrativeness of mathematics stood out in the clearest contrast to the uncertainty, the obscurity, of all other knowledge. And to them, as to all before the days of Kant, it seemed beyond doubt that the method of mathematics consists in the analysis of notions, and in their synthesis through the medium of axioms, which are true because identical statements; while the notions are true because clear and distinct.

And yet the method led Leibniz in a very different direction. One of the fundamental doctrines, for example, of Leibniz is the existence everywhere of minute and obscure perceptions, — which are of the greatest importance, but of which we, at least, can never have distinct consciousness. How is this factor of his thought, which almost approaches mysticism, to be reconciled with the statements just made? It is found in the different application which is made of the method. The object of Descartes is the *erection of a new structure of truth* upon a *tabula rasa* of all former doctrines. The object of Leibniz is the *interpretation of an old body of truth* by a method which shall reveal it in its clearest light. Descartes and Spinoza are "rationalists" both in their method and results. Leibniz is a "rationalist" in his method; but his application of the method is everywhere controlled by historic considerations. It is, I think, impossible to overemphasize this fact. Descartes was profoundly convinced that past thought had gone wrong, and that its results were worthless. Leibniz was as profoundly convinced that its instincts had been right, and that the general idea of the world which it gave was correct. Leibniz would have given the heartiest assent to Goethe's saying, "Das Wahre war schon längst gefunden." It was out of the question, then, that he should use the new method in any other than an interpreting way to bring out in a connected system and unity the true meaning of the subject-matter.

So much of generality for the method of Leibniz. The positive substance of doctrine which he developed under scientific influence affords matter for more discussion. Of the three influences which meet us here, two are still Cartesian; the third is from the new science of biology, although not yet answering to that name. These three influences are, in order: the idea that nature is to be explained mechanically; that this is to be brought about through the application of mathematics; and, from biology, the idea that all change is of the nature of continuous growth or unfolding. Let us consider each in this order.

What is meant by the mechanical explanation of nature? To answer a question thus baldly put, we must recall the kind of explanations which had satisfied the scholastic men of science. They had been explanations which, however true, Leibniz says, as general principles, do not touch the details of the matter. The explanations of natural facts had been found in general principles, in substantial forces, in occult essences, in native faculties. Now, the first contention of the founders of the modern scientific movement was that such general considerations are not verifiable, and that if they are, they are entirely aside from the point, — they fail to explain any given fact. Explanation must always consist in discovering an immediate connection between some fact and some co-existing or preceding fact. Explanation does not consist in referring a fact to a general power, it consists in referring it to an antecedent whose existence is its necessary condition. It was not left till the times of Mr. Huxley to poke fun at those who would explain some concrete phenomenon by reference to an abstract principle ending in —ity. Leibniz has his word to say about those who would account for the movements of a watch by reference to a principle of horologity, and of mill-stones by a fractive principle.

Mechanical explanation consists, accordingly, in making out an actual connection between two existing facts. But this does not say very much. A connection of what kind? In the first place, a connection of the same order as the facts observed. If we are explaining corporeal phenomena, we must find a corporeal link; if we are explaining phenomena of motion, we must find a connection of motion. In one of his first philosophical works Leibniz, in taking the mechanical position, states what he means by it. In the "Confession of Nature against the Atheists" he says that it must be confessed to those who have revived the corpuscular theory of Democritus and Epicurus, to Galileo, Bacon, Gassendi, Hobbes, and Descartes, that in explaining material phenomena recourse is to be had neither to God nor to any other incorporeal thing, form, or quality, but that all things are to be explained from the nature of matter and its qualities, especially from their magnitude, figure, and motion. The physics of Descartes, to which was especially due the spread of mechanical notions, virtually postulated the problem: given a homogeneous quantity of matter, endowed only with extension and mobility, to account for all material phenomena. Leibniz accepts this mechanical view without reserve.

What has been said suggests the bearing of mathematics in this connection. Extension and mobility may be treated by mathematics. It is indeed the business of the geometer to give us an analysis of figured space, to set before us all possible combinations which can arise, assuming extension only. The higher analysis sets before us the results which inevitably follow if we suppose a moving point or any system of movements. Mathematics is thus the essential tool for treating physical phenomena as just defined. But it is more. The mechanical explanation of Nature not only requires such a development of mathematics as will make it applicable to the interpretation of physical facts, but the employment of mathematics is necessary for the very discovery of these facts. Exact observation was the necessity of the growing physical science; and exact observation means such as will answer the question, *How much?* Knowledge of nature depends upon our ability to *measure* her processes, — that is, to reduce distinctions of quality to those of quantity. The only assurance that we can finally have that two facts are connected in such a way as to fulfil the requirements of scientific research, is that there is a complete quantitative connection between them, so that one can be regarded as the other transformed. The advance of physical science from the days of Copernicus to the present has consisted, therefore, on one hand, in a development of mathematics which has made it possible to apply it in greater and greater measure to the discussion and formulation of the results of experiment, and to deduce laws which, when interpreted physically, will give new knowledge of fact; and, on the other, to multiply, sharpen, and make precise all sorts of devices by which the processes of nature may be measured. The explanation of nature by natural processes; the complete application of mathematics to nature, — these are the two thoughts which, so far, we have seen to be fundamental to the development of the philosophy of Leibniz.

The third factor, and that which brings Leibniz nearer, perhaps, our own day than either of the others, is the growth of physiological science. Swammerdam, Malpighi, Leewenhoek, — these are names which occur and recur in the pages of Leibniz. Indeed, he appears to be the first of that now long line of modern philosophers to be profoundly influenced by the conception of life and the categories of organic growth. Descartes concerned himself indeed with physiological problems, but it was only with a view to applying mechanical principles. The idea of the vital unity of all organs of the body might seem to be attractive to one filled with the notion of the unity of all in God, and yet Spinoza shows no traces of the influence of the organic conception. Not until Kant's famous definition of organism do we see another philosopher moved by an attempt to comprehend the categories of living structure.

But it is the idea of organism, of life, which is radical to the thought of Leibniz. I do not think, however, that it can truly be said that he was led to the idea simply from the state of physiological investigation at that time. Rather, he had already learned to think of the world as organic through and through, and found in the results of biology confirmations, apt illustrations of a truth of which he was already thoroughly convinced. His writings show that there were two aspects of biological science which especially interested him. One was the simple fact of organism itself, — the fact of the various activities of different organs occurring in complete harmony for one end. This presented three notions very dear to the mind of Leibniz, or rather three moments of the same idea, — the factors of activity, of unity brought about by co-ordinated action, and of an end which reveals the meaning of the activity and is the ideal expression of the unity. The physiologists of that day were also occupied with the problem of growth. The generalization that all is developed *ab ovo* was just receiving universal attention. The question which thrust itself upon science for solution was the mode by which ova, apparently homogeneous in structure, developed into the various forms of the organic kingdom. The answer given was "evolution." But evolution had not the meaning which the term has to-day. By evolution was meant that the whole complex structure of man, for example, was virtually contained in the germ, and that the apparent phenomenon of growth was not the addition of anything from without, but simply the unfolding and magnifying of that already existing. It was the doctrine which afterwards gave way to the epigenesis theory of Wolff, according to which growth is not mere unfolding or unwrapping, but progressive differentiation. The "evolution" theory was the scientific theory of the times, however, and was warmly espoused by Leibniz. To him, as we shall see hereafter, it seemed to give a key which would unlock one of the problems of the universe.

Such, then, were the three chief generalizations which Leibniz found current, and which most deeply affected him. But what use did he make of them? He did not become a philosopher by letting them lie dormant in his mind, nor by surrendering himself passively to them till he could mechanically apply them everywhere. He was a philosopher only in virtue of the active attitude which his mind took towards them. He could not simply accept them at their face-value; he must ask after the source of their value, the royal stamp of meaning which made them a circulatory medium. That is to say, he had to interpret these ideas, to see what they mean, and what is the basis of their validity.

Not many men have been so conscious of just the bearings of their own ideas and of their source as was he. He often allows us a direct glimpse into the method of his thinking, and nowhere more than when he says: "Those who give themselves up to the details of science usually despise abstract and general researches. Those who go into universal principles rarely care for particular facts. But I equally esteem both." Leibniz, in other words, was equally interested in the application of scientific principles to the explanation of the details of natural phenomena, and in the bearing and meaning of the principles themselves, — a rare combination, indeed, but one, which existing, stamps the genuine philosopher. Leibniz substantially repeats this idea when he says: "Particular effects must be explained mechanically; but the general principles of physics and mathematics depend upon metaphysics." And again: "All occurs mechanically; but the mechanical principle is not to be explained from material and mathematical considerations, but it flows from a higher and a metaphysical source."

As a man of science, Leibniz might have stopped short with the ideas of mechanical law, of the application of mathematics, and of the continuity of development. As a philosopher he could not. There are some scientific men to whom it always seems a perversion of their principles to attempt to carry them any beyond their application to the details of the subject. They look on in a bewildered and protesting attitude when there is suggested the necessity of any further inquiry. Or perhaps they dogmatically deny the possibility of any such investigation, and as dogmatically assume the sufficiency of their principles for the decision of all possible problems. But bewildered fear and dogmatic assertion are equally impotent to fix arbitrary limits to human thought. Wherever there is a subject that has meaning, there is a field which appeals to mind, and the mind will not cease its endeavors till it has made out what that meaning is, and has made it out in its entirety. So the three principles already spoken of were but the starting-points, the stepping-stones of Leibniz's philosophic thought. While to physical science they are solutions, to philosophy they are problems; and as such Leibniz recognized them. What solution did he give?

So far as the principle of mechanical explanation is concerned, the clew is given by considering the factor upon which he laid most emphasis, namely, motion. Descartes had said that the essence of the physical world is extension. "Not so," replied Leibniz; "it is motion." These answers mark two typical ways of regarding nature. According to one, nature is something essentially rigid and static; whatever change in it occurs, is a change of form, of arrangement, an external modification. According to the other, nature is something essentially dynamic and active. Change according to law is its very essence. Form, arrangement are only the results of this internal principle. And so to Leibniz, extension and the spatial aspects of physical existence were only secondary, they were phenomenal. The primary, the real fact was motion.

The considerations which led him to this conclusion are simple enough. It is the fact already mentioned, that explanation always consists in reducing phenomena to a law of motion which connects them. Descartes himself had not succeeded in writing his physics without everywhere using the conception of motion. But motion cannot be got out of the idea of extension. Geometry will not give us activity. What is this, except virtually to admit the insufficiency of purely statical conceptions? Leibniz found himself confirmed in this position by the fact that the more logical of the followers of Descartes had recognized that motion is a superfluous intruder, if extension be indeed the essence of matter, and therefore had been obliged to have recourse to the immediate activity of God as the cause of all changes. But this, as Leibniz said, was simply to give up the very idea of mechanical explanation, and to fall back into the purely general explanations of scholasticism.

This is not the place for a detailed exposition of the ideas of Leibniz regarding matter, motion, and extension. We need here only recognize that he saw in motion the final reality of the physical universe. But what about motion? To many, perhaps the majority, of minds to-day it seems useless or absurd, or both, to ask any question about motion. It is simply an ultimate *fact*, to which all other facts are to be reduced. We are so familiar with it as a solution of all physical problems that we are confused, and fail to recognize it when it appears in the guise of a problem. But, I repeat, philosophy cannot stop with facts, however ultimate. It must also know something about the meaning, the significance, in short the ideal bearing, of facts. From the point of view of philosophy, motion has a certain function in the economy of the universe; it is, as Aristotle saw, something ideal.

The name of Aristotle suggests the principles which guided Leibniz in his interpretation of the fact of motion. The thought of Aristotle moves about the two poles of potentiality and actuality. Potentiality is not *mere* capacity; it is being in an undeveloped, imperfect stage. Actuality is, as the word suggests, activity. Anything is potential in so far as it does not manifest itself in action; it is actual so far as it does thus show forth its being. Now, movement, or change in its most general sense, is that by which the potential comes to the realization of its nature, and functions as an activity. Motion, then, is not an ultimate fact, but is subordinate. It exists for an end. It is that by which existence realizes its idea; that is, its proper type of action.

Now Leibniz does not formally build upon these distinctions; and yet he is not very far removed from Aristotle. Motion, he is never weary of repeating, means force, means energy, means activity. To say that the essence of nature is motion, is to say that the natural world finally introduces us to the supremacy of action. Reality is activity. *Substance c'est l'action.* That is the key-note and the battle-cry of the Leibnizian philosophy. Motion is that by which being expresses its nature, fulfils its purpose, reveals its idea. In short, the specific scientific conception of motion is by Leibniz transformed into the philosophic conception of force, of activity. In motion he sees evidence of the fact that the universe is radically dynamic.

In the applicability of mathematics to the interpretation of nature Leibniz finds witness to the continuity and order of the world. We have become so accustomed to the fact that mathematics may be directly employed for the discussion and formulation of physical investigations that we forget what is implied in it. It involves the huge assumption that the world answers to reason; so that whatever the mind finds to be ideally true may be taken for granted to be physically true also. But in those days, when the correlation of the laws of the world and the laws of mathematical reasoning was a fresh discovery, this aspect of the case could not be easily lost sight of.

In fact it was this correlation which filled the *Zeitgeist* of the sixteenth century with the idea that it had a new organ for the penetration of nature, a new sense for learning its meaning. Descartes gives the following as the origin of his philosophy: "The long chains of simple and easy reasons which geometers employ, even in their most complex demonstrations, made me fancy that all things which are the objects of human knowledge are *similarly interdependent*." To Leibniz also mathematics seemed to give a clew to the order, the interdependence, the harmonious relations, of the world.

In this respect the feeling of Plato that God geometrizes found an echoing response in Leibniz. But the latter would hardly have expressed it in the same way. He would have preferred to say that God everywhere uses the infinitesimal calculus. In the applicability of the calculus to the discussion of physical facts, Leibniz saw two truths reflected, — that everything that occurs has its reason, its dependent connection upon something else, and that all is continuous and without breaks. While the formal principles of his logic are those of identity and contradiction, his real principles are those of sufficient reason and of continuity. Nature never makes leaps; everything in nature has a sufficient reason why it is as it is : these are the philosophic generalizations which Leibniz finds hidden in the applicability of mathematics to physical science. Reason finds itself everywhere expressed in nature; and the law of reason is unity in diversity, continuity.

Let us say, in a word, that the correlation between the laws of mathematics and of physics is the evidence of the rational character of nature. Nature may be reduced to motions; and motions can be understood only as force, activity. But the laws which connect motions are fundamentally mathematical laws, — laws of reason. Hence force, activity, can be understood only as rational, as spiritual. Nature is thus seen to mean Activity, and Activity is seen to mean Intelligence. Furthermore, as the fundamental law of intelligence is the production of difference in unity, the primary law of physical change must be the manifestation of this unity in difference, — or, as Leibniz interpreted it, continuity. In nature there are no breaks, neither of quantity nor of quality nor of relationship. The full force of this law we shall see later.

Such an idea can hardly be distinguished from the idea of growth or development; one passes naturally into the other. Thus it is equally proper to say that the third scientific influence, the conception of organism and growth, is dominant in the Leibnizian thought, or that this is swallowed up and absorbed in the grand idea of continuity. The law of animal and vegetable life and the law of the universe are identified. The substance of the universe is activity; the law of the universe is interdependence. What is this but to say that the universe is an organic whole? Its activity is the manifestation of life, — nay, it is life. The laws of its activity reveal that continuity of development, that harmony ot inter-relation, which are everywhere the marks of life. The final and fundamental notion, therefore, by which Leibniz interprets the laws of physics and mathematics is that of Life. This is his regnant category. It is "that higher and metaphysical source" from which the very existence and principles of mechanism flow. The perpetual and ubiquitous presence of motion reveals the pulsations of Life; the correlation, the rationality, of these motions indicate the guiding presence of Life. This idea is the alpha and omega of his philosophy.

CHAPTER III.

THE PROBLEM, AND ITS SOLUTION.

LEIBNIZ, like every great man, absorbed into himself the various thoughts of his time, and in absorbing transformed them. He brought into a focus of brilliancy the diffused lights of truth shining here and there. He summed up in a pregnant and comprehensive category the scattered principles of his age. Yet we are not to suppose that Leibniz considered these various ideas one by one, and then patched them into an artificial unity of thought. Philosophies are not manufactured piecemeal out of isolated and fragmentary thoughts; they grow from a single root, absorbing from their environment whatever of sustenance offers itself, and maturing in one splendid fruit of spiritual truth. It is convenient, indeed, to isolate various phases of truth, and consider them as distinct forces working to shape one final product, and as a convenient artifice it is legitimate. But it answers to no process actually occurring. Leibniz never surrendered his personal unity, and out of some one root-conception grew all his ideas. The principles of his times were not separate forces acting upon him, they were the foods of which he selected and assimilated such as were fitted to nourish his one great conception.

But it is more than a personal unity which holds together the thinking of a philosopher. There is the unity of the problem, which the philosopher has always before him, and in which all particular ideas find their unity. All else issues from this and merges into it. The various influences which we have seen affecting Leibniz, therefore, got their effectiveness from the relation which he saw them bear to the final problem of all thought. This is the inquiry after the unity of experience, if we look at it from the side of the subject; the unity of reality, if we put it from the objective side. Yet each age states this problem in its own way, because it sees it in the light of some difficulty which has recently arisen in consciousness. At one time, the question is as to the relation of the one to the many; at another, of the relation of the sensible to the intelligible world; at another, of the relation of the individual to the universal. And this last seems to have been the way in which it specifically presented itself to Leibniz. This way of stating it was developed, though apparently without adequate realization of its meaning, by the philosophy of scholasticism. It stated the problem as primarily a logical question, — the relation of genera, of species, of individuals to each other. And the school-boy, made after the stamp of literary tradition, knows that there were two parties among the Schoolmen, — the Realists, and the Nominalists; one asserting, the other denying, the objective reality of universals. To regard this discussion as useless, is to utter the condemnation of philosophy, and to relegate the foundation of science to the realm of things not to be inquired into. To say that it is an easy matter to decide, is to assume the decision with equal ease of all the problems that have vexed the thought of humanity. To us it seems easy because we have bodily incorporated into our thinking the results of both the realistic and the nominalistic doctrines, without attempting to reconcile them, or even being conscious of the necessity of reconciliation. We assert in one breath that the individual is alone real, and in the next assert that only those forms of consciousness which represent something in the universe are to be termed knowledge. At one moment we say that universals are creations of the individual mind, and at the next pass on to talk of laws of nature, or even of a reign of law. In other words, we have learned to regard both the individual and the universal as real, and thus ignoring the problem, think we have solved it.

But to Leibniz the problem presented itself neither as a logical question, nor yet as one whose solution might be taken for granted. On the contrary, it was just this question: How shall we conceive the individual to be related to the universe? which seemed to him to be the nerve of the philosophic problem, the question whose right answer would solve the problems of religion, of morals, of the basis of science, as well as of the nature of reality. The importance of just this way of putting the question had been rendered evident by the predecessors and contemporaries of Leibniz, especially by Descartes, Spinoza, and Locke. His more specific relations to the last-named will occupy us hereafter; at present we must notice how the question stood at the hands of Descartes and Spinoza.

Descartes had separated the individual from the universal. His philosophy began and ended with a dualism. I have just said that the problem of philosophy is the unity of experience. Yet we find that there have been thinkers, and those of the first rank, who have left the matter without discovering any ultimate unity, or rather who have made it the burden of their contention that we cannot explain the world without at least two disparate principles. But if we continue to look at the matter in this historical way, we shall see that this dualism has always been treated by the successors of such a philosopher, not as a solution, but as a deeper statement of the problem. It is the function of dualistic philosophies to re-state the question in a new and more significant way. There are times when the accepted unity of thought is seen to be inadequate and superficial. Men are thrashing old straw, and paying themselves with ideas which have lost their freshness and their timeliness. There then arises a philosopher who goes deep, beyond the superficial unity, and who discovers the untouched problem. His it is to assert the true meaning of the question, which has been unseen or evaded. The attitude of dualism is thus always necessary, but never final. Its value is not in any solution, but in the generality and depth of the problem which it proposes, and which incites thought to the discovery of a unity of equal depth and comprehensiveness.

Except for Descartes, then, we should not be conscious of the gulf that yawns between the individual mind and the universe in front of it. He presented the opposition as between mind and matter. The essence of the former is thought; of the latter, extension. The conceptions are disparate and opposed. No interaction is possible. His disciples, more consistent than their master, called in a *deus ex machina*, — the miraculous intervention of God, — in order to account for the appearance of reciprocal action between the universe of matter and the thinking individual. Thus they in substance admitted the relation between them to be scientifically inexplicable, and had recourse to the supernatural. The individual does not act upon the universe to produce, destroy, or alter the arrangement of anything. But upon the *occasion* of his volition God produces a corresponding material change. The world does not act upon the soul of the individual to produce thoughts or sensations. God, upon *occasion* of the external affection, brings them into being. With such thoroughness Descartes performed his task of separation. Yet the introduction of the *deus ex machina* only complicated the problem; it introduced a third factor where two were already too many. What is the relation of God to Mind and to Matter? Is it simply a third somewhat, equally distinct from both, or does it contain both within itself?

Spinoza attempted to solve the problem in the latter sense. He conceived God to be the one substance of the universe, possessing the two known attributes of thought and matter. These attributes are one in God; indeed, he is their unity. This is the sole legitimate outcome of the Cartesian problem stated as Descartes would have it stated. It overcomes the absoluteness of the dualism by discovering a common and fundamental unity, and at the same time takes the subject out of the realm of the miraculous. For the solution works both ways. It affects the nature of God, as well as of extension and thought. It presents him to us, not as a supernatural being, but as the unity of thought and extension. In knowing these as they are, we know God as he is. Spinoza, in other words, uses the conception of God in a different way from the Cartesians. The latter had treated him as the God of theology, — a being supernatural; Spinoza uses the conception as a scientific one, and speaks of *Deus sive Natura.*

Leibniz recognized the unphilosophic character of the recourse to a *deus ex machina* as clearly as Spinoza, and yet did not accept his solution. To find out why he did not is the problem of the historian of thought. The one cause which stands out above all others is that in the unity of Spinoza all difference, all distinction, is lost. All particular existences, whether things or persons, are *modes* of extension and thought. Their *apparent* existence is due to the imagination, which is the source of belief in particular things. When considered as they really are, — that is, by the understanding, — they vanish. The one substance, with its two unchanging attributes of thought and extension, alone remains. If it is a philosophic error to give a solution which permits of no unity, is it not equally a philosophic error to give one which denies difference? So it seemed to Leibniz. The problem is to reconcile difference in unity, not to swallow up difference in a blank oneness, — to reconcile the individual with the universe, not to absorb him.

The unsatisfactoriness of the solution appears if we look at it from another side. Difference implies change, while a unity in which all variety is lost implies quiescence. Change is as much an illusion of imagination to Spinoza as is variety. The One Reality is permanent. How repugnant the conception of a static universe was to Leibniz we have already learned. Spinoza fails to satisfy Leibniz, therefore, because he does not allow the conceptions of individuality and of activity. He presents a unity in which all distinction of individuals is lost, and in which there is no room for change. But Spinoza certainly presented the problem more clearly to Leibniz, and revealed more definitely the conditions of its solution. The search is henceforth for a unity which shall avoid the irresolvable dualism of Descartes, and yet shall allow free play to the principles of individuality and of activity. There must be, in short, a universe to which the individual bears a real yet independent relation. What is this unity? The answer, in the phraseology of Leibniz, is the *monad*. Spinoza would be right, said Leibniz, were it not for the existence of monads. I know there are some who have done Leibniz the honor of supposing that this is his way of saying, "Spinoza is wrong because I am right;" but I cannot help thinking that the saying has a somewhat deeper meaning. What, then, is the nature of the monad? The answer to this question takes us back to the point where the discussion of the question was left at the end of chapter second. The nature of the monad is life. The monad is the spiritual activity which lives in absolute harmony with an infinite number of other monads.

Let us first consider the reasons of Leibniz for conceiving the principle of unity as spiritual. Primarily it is because it is impossible to conceive of a unity which is material. In the sensible world there is no unity. There are, indeed, aggregations, collections, which seem like unities; but the very fact that these are aggregations shows that the unity is factitious. It is the very nature of matter to be infinitely divisible: to say this is to deny the existence of any true principle of unity. The world of nature is the world of space and time; and where in space or time shall we find a unity where we may rest?

Every point in space, every moment in time, points beyond itself. It refers to a totality of which it is but a part, or, rather, a limitation. If we add resistance, we are not better situated. We have to think of something which resists; and to this something we must attribute extension, — that is to say, difference, plurality. Nor can we find any resistance which is absolute and final. There may be a body which is undivided, and which resists all energy now acting upon it; but we cannot frame an intelligible idea of a body which is absolutely indivisible. To do so is to think of a body out of all relation to existing forces, something absolutely isolated; while the forces of nature are always relative to one another. That which resists does so in comparison with some opposing energy. The absolutely indivisible, on the other hand, would be that which could not be brought into comparison with other forces; it would not have any of the attributes of force as we know it. In a word, whatever exists in nature is relative in space, in time, and in qualities to all else. It is made what it is by virtue of the totality of its relations to the universe; it has no ultimate principle of self-subsistent unity in it.

Nor do we fare better if we attempt to find unity in the world of nature as a whole. Nature has its existence as a whole in space and time. Indeed, it is only a way of expressing the totality of phenomena of space and time. It is a mere aggregate, a collection. Its very essence is plurality, difference. It is divisible without limit, and each of its divisions has as good a right to be called one as the whole from which it is broken off. We shall consider hereafter Leibniz's idea of infinity; but it is easy to see that he must deny any true infinity to nature. An ultimate whole made up of parts is a contradictory conception; and the idea of a quantitative infinite is equally so. Quantity means number, measure, limitation. We may not be able to assign number to the totality of occurrences in nature, nor to measure her every event. This shows that nature is indefinitely greater than any *assignable* quantity; but it does not remove her from the category of quantity. As long as the world is conceived as that existing in space and time, it is conceived as that which has to be measured. As we saw in the last chapter, the heart of the mechanical theory of the world is in the application of mathematics to it. Since quantity and mathematics are correlative terms, the natural world cannot be conceived as infinite or as an ultimate unity.

In short, Leibniz urges and suggests in one form and another those objections to the mechanical theory of reality which later German philosophers have made us so familiar with. The objections are indeed varied in statement, but they all come to the impossibility of finding any unity, any wholeness, anything except plurality and partiality in that which is externally conditioned, — as everything is in nature.

But the reasons as thus stated are rather negative than positive. They show why the ultimate unity cannot be conceived as material, rather than why it must be conceived as spiritual. The immediate evidence of its spiritual nature Leibniz finds in the perception of the one unity directly known to us, — the "me," the conscious principle within, which reveals itself as an active force, and as truly one, since not a spatial or temporal existence. And this evidence he finds confirmed by the fact that whatever unity material phenomena appear to have comes to them through their perception by the soul. Whatever the mind grasps in one act, is manifested as one.

But it is not in any immediate certainty of fact that Leibniz finds the best or completest demonstration of the spiritual nature of the ultimate unity. This is found in the use which can be made of the hypothesis. The truest witness to the spiritual character of reality is found in the capacity of this principle to comprehend and explain the facts of experience. With this conception the reason of things can be ascertained, and light introduced into what were otherwise a confused obscurity. And, indeed, this is the only sufficient proof of any doctrine. It is not what comes before the formulation of a theory which proves it; it is not the facts which suggest it, or the processes which lead up to it: it is what comes after the formation of the theory, — the uses that it can be put to; the facts which it will render significant. The whole philosophy of Leibniz in its simplicity, width, and depth, is the real evidence of the truth of his philosophical principle.

The monad, then, is a spiritual unity; it is individualized life. Unity, activity, individuality, are synonymous terms in the vocabulary of Leibniz. Every unity is a true substance, containing within itself the source and law of its own activity. It is that which is internally determined to action. It is to be conceived after the analogy of the soul. It is an indivisible unity, like "that particular something in us which thinks, apperceives and wills, and distinguishes us in a way of its own from whatever else thinks and wills." Against Descartes, therefore, Leibniz stands for the principle of unity; against Spinoza, he upholds the doctrine of individuality, of diversity, of multiplicity. And the latter principle is as important in his thought as the former. Indeed, they are inseparable. The individual is the true unity. There is an infinite number of these individuals, each distinct from every other. The law of specification, of distinction, runs through the universe. Two beings cannot be alike. They are not individualized merely by their different positions in space or time; duration and extension, on the contrary, are, as we have seen, principles of relativity, of connection. Monads are specified by an internal principle. Their distinct individuality is constituted by their distinct law of activity. Leibniz will not have a philosophy of abstract unity, representing the universe as simple only, he will have a philosophy equal to the diversity, the manifold wealth of variety, in the universe. This is only to say that he will be faithful to his fundamental notion, — that of Life. Life does not mean a simple unity like a mathematical one, it means a unity which is the harmony of the interplay of diverse organs, each following its own law and having its own function. When Leibniz says, God willed to have more monads rather than fewer, the expression is indeed one of *naïveté*, but the thought is one of unexplored depth. It is the thought that Leibniz repeats when he says, "Those who would reduce all things to modifications of one universal substance do not have sufficient regard to the *order*, the *harmony* of reality." Leibniz applies here, as everywhere, the principle of continuity, which is unity in and through diversity, not the principle of bare oneness. There is a kingdom of monads, a realm truly infinite, composed of individual unities or activities in an absolute continuity. Leibniz was one of the first, if not the first, to use just the expression "uniformity of nature;" but even here he explains that it means "uniform in variety, one in principle, but varied in manifestation." The world is to be as rich as possible. This is simply to say that distinct individuality as well as ultimate unity is a law of reality.

But has not Leibniz fallen into a perilous position? In avoiding the monotone of unity which characterizes the thought of Spinoza, has he not fallen into a lawless variety of multiplicity, infinitely less philosophic than even the dualism of Descartes, since it has an infinity of ultimate principles instead of only two? If Spinoza sacrificed the individual to the universe, has not Leibniz, in his desire toemphasize the individual, gone to the other extreme? Apparently we are introduced to a universe that is a mere aggregate of an infinite multiplicity of realities, each independent of every other. Such a universe would not be a universe. It would be a chaos of disorder and conflict. We come, therefore, to a consideration of the relation between these individual monads and the universe. We have to discover what lifts the monads out of their isolation and bestows upon them that stamp of universality which makes it possible for them to enter into the coherent structure of reality: in a word, what is the universal content which the monad in its formal individuality bears and manifests?

The way in which the question has just been stated suggests the Leibnizian answer. The monad, indeed, in its form is thoroughly individual, having its own unique mode of activity; but its content, that which this activity manifests, is not peculiar to it as an individual, but is the substance or law of the universe. It is the very nature of the monad to be representative. Its activity consists in picturing or reproducing those relations which make up the world of reality. In a conscious soul, the ability thus to represent the world is called "perception," and thus Leibniz attributes perception to all the monads. This is not to be understood as a conscious representation of reality to itself (for this the term "apperception" is reserved), but it signifies that the very essence of the monad is to produce states which are not its own peculiar possessions, but which reflect the facts and relations of the universe. Leibniz never wearies in finding new ways to express this purely representative character of the monad. The monads are little souls; they are mirrors of the world; they are concentrations of the universe, each expressing it in its own way; borrowing a term from scholasticism, they are "substantial forms." They are substantial, for they are independent unities; they are forms, because the term "form" expresses, in Aristotelian phraseology, the type or law of some class of phenomena. The monad is an individual, but its whole content, its objectivity or reality, is the summation of the universe which it represents. It is individual, but whatever marks it as actual is some reproduction of the world. His reconciliation of the principles of individuality and universality is contained in the following words: "Each monad contains within itself an order corresponding to that of the universe,—indeed, the monads represent the universe in an infinity of ways, all different, and all true, thus multiplying the universe as many times as is possible, approaching the divine as near as may be, and giving the world all the perfection of which it is capable." The monad is individual, for it represents reality in its own way, from its own point of view. It is universal, for its whole content is the order of the universe.

New light is thus thrown upon the former statement that reality is activity, that the measure of a being is the action which it puts forth. That statement is purely formal. It leaves the kind of activity and its law wholly undetermined. But this relation of "representativeness" which we have discovered gives definiteness. It is the law of the monad's action to mirror, to reflect, the universe; its changes follow each other so as to bring about this reflection in the completest degree possible. The monad is literally the many in the one; it is the answer to the inquiry of Greek philosophy. The many are not present by way of participation in some underlying essence, not yet as statically possessed by the one, as attributes are sometimes supposed to inhere in a substratum. The "many" is the manifestation of the activity of the "one." The one and the many are related as form and content in an organic unity, which is activity. The essence of a substance, says Leibniz, consists in that regular tendency of action by which its phenomena follow one another in a certain order; and that order, as he repeatedly states, is the order in which the universe itself is arranged.

The activity of a monad may be advantageously compared to that of a supposed atom, granting, for the sake of the illustration, that there is such a thing. Each is in a state of change: the atom changes its place, the monad its representation, and each in the simplest and most uniform way that its conditions permit. How, then, is there such a similarity, such a monotony, in the change of an atom, and such variety and complexity in the change of a monad?

It is because the atom has merely parts, or external variety, while the monad has an internal variety. Multiplicity is organically wrought into its very being. It has an *essential* relation to all things in the universe; and to say that this relation is essential, is to say that it is one which constitutes its very content, its being. Hence the cause of the changes of the monad, of their variety and complexity, is one with the cause of the richness, the profusion, the regulated variety of change in the universe itself. While we have employed a comparison with atoms, this very comparison may serve to show us the impossibility of atoms as they are generally defined by the physicist turned philosopher. Atoms have no internal and essential relation to the world; they have no internal connection with any one thing in the world: and what is this but to say that they do not enter anywhere into the structure of the world? By their very conception they are forever aliens, banished from any share or lot in the realm of reality. The idea which Leibniz never lets go, the idea which he always accentuates, is, then, the idea of an individual activity which in its continual change manifests as its own internal content and reality that reality and those laws of connection which make up the world itself.

We are thus introduced naturally to the conception which plays so large a part in the Leibnizian philosophy, that of pre-established harmony. This term simply names the fact, which we see to be fundamental with Leibniz, — the fact that, while the form of every monad is individuality, a unique principle of action, its content is universal, the very being and laws of the world. For we must now notice more explicitly what has been wrapped up in the idea all along. There is no direct influence of monads upon each other. One cannot affect another causally. There is no actual interaction of one upon another. Expressed in that figurative language which was ever natural to Leibniz, the monads have no windows by which anything can get in or out. This follows, of course, from the mutual independence and individuality of the monads. They are a true democracy, in which each citizen has sovereignty. To admit external influences acting upon them is to surrender their independence, to deny their sovereignty. But we must remember the other half. This democracy is not after the Platonic conception of democracy, in which each does as it pleases, and in which there is neither order nor law, but the extremest assertion of individuality. What each sovereign citizen of the realm of reality expresses is precisely law. Each is an embodiment in its own way of the harmony, the order, of the whole kingdom. Each is sovereign because it is dynamic law, — law which is no longer abstract, but has realized itself in life. Thus another way of stating the doctrine of pre-established harmony is the unity of freedom and necessity. Each monad is free because it is individual, because it follows the law of its own activity unhindered, unretarded, by others; it is self-determined. But it is self-determined to show forth the order, the harmony, of the universe. There is nothing of caprice, of peculiarity, in the content of the monad. It shows forth order; it is organized by law; it reveals the necessary connections which constitute the universe. The pre-established harmony is the unity of the individual and the universe; it is the organic oneness of freedom and necessity.

We see still further what it means when we learn that it is by this conception that Leibniz reconciles the conceptions of physical and final causation. There is no principle closer to the thought of Leibniz than that of the equal presence and efficiency everywhere of both physical and final causes. Every fact which occurs is susceptible of a mechanical and of a rational explanation. It is necessarily connected with preceding states, and it has a necessary end which it is fulfilling. The complete meaning of this principle will meet us hereafter; at present we must notice that it is one form of the doctrine of pre-established harmony. All things have an end because they form parts of one system; everything that occurs looks forward to something else and prepares the way for it, and yet it is itself mechanically conditioned by its antecedents. This is only another way of saying that there is complete harmony between all beings in the universe; so that each monad in fulfilling the law of its own existence contributes to the immanent significance of the universe. The monads are co-ordinated in such a way that they express a common idea. There is a plan common to all, in which each has its own place. All are making towards one goal, expressing one purpose. The universe is an organism; and Leibniz would have applied to it the words which Milne-Edwards applied to the human organism, as I find them quoted by Lewes: "In the organism everything seems to be calculated with one determined result in view; and the harmony of the parts does not result from the influence which they exert upon one another, but from their co-ordination under the rule of a common force, a preconceived plan, a pre-existent force." That is to say, the universe is teleological, both as a whole and in its parts; for there is a common idea animating it and expressed by it; it is mechanical, for this idea is realized and manifested by the outworking of forces.

It ought to be evident even from this imperfect sketch that the Leibnizian theory of pre-established harmony is not that utterly artificial and grotesque doctrine which it is sometimes represented to be. The phrase "pre-established harmony" is, strictly speaking, tautologous. The term "pre-established" is superfluous. It means "existent." There is no real harmony which is not existent or pre-established. An accidental harmony is a contradiction in terms. It means a chaotic cosmos, an unordered order, a lawless law, or whatever else is nonsensical.

Harmony, in short, means relation, means connection, means subordination and co-ordination, means adjustment, means a variety, which yet is one. The Leibnizian doctrine is not a factitious product of his imagination, nor is it a mechanical scheme for reconciling a problem which has no existence outside of the bewildered brains of philosophers. It is an expression of the fact that the universe is one of order, of continuity, of unity; it is the accentuating of this doctrine so that the very essence of reality is found in this ordered combination; it is the special application of this principle to the solution of many of the problems which "the mind of man is apt to run into," — the questions of the relation of the individual and the universal, of freedom and necessity, of the physical and material, of the teleological and mechanical. We may not be contented with the doctrine as he presents it, we may think it to be rather a summary and highly concentrated statement of the problem than its solution, or we may object to details in the carrying out of the doctrine. But we cannot deny that it is a genuine attempt to meet a genuine problem, and that it contains some, if not all, of the factors required for its adequate solution. To Leibniz must remain the glory of being the thinker to seize upon the perfect unity and order of the universe as its essential characteristic, and of arranging his thoughts with a view to discovering and expressing it.

We have but to notice one point more, and our task is done so far as it serves to make plain the standpoint from which Leibniz criticised Locke. There is, we have seen, the greatest possible continuity and complexity in the realm of monads.

There is no break, quantitative nor qualitative. It follows that the human soul has no gulf set between it and what we call nature. It is only the highest, that is to say the most active and the most representative, of all monads. It stands, indeed, at the head of the scale, but not outside it. From the monad which reveals its presence in that stone which with blinded eyes we call dead, through that which acts in the plant, in the animal, up to that of man, there is no chasm, no interruption. Nay, man himself is but one link in the chain of spiritual beings which ends only in God. All monads are souls; the soul of man is a monad which represents the universe more distinctly and adequately. The law which is enfolded in the lower monads is developed in it and forms a part of its conscious activity. The universe, which is confusedly mirrored by the perception of the lower monad, is clearly brought out in the conscious apperception of man. The stone is representative of the whole world. An all-knowing intelligence might read in it relations to every other fact in the world, might see exemplified the past history of the world, and prefigured the events to come. For the stone is not an isolated existence, it is an inter-organic member of a system. Change the slightest fact in the world, and in some way it is affected. The law of the universe is one of completed reciprocity, and this law must be mirrored in every existence of the universe. Increase the activity, the representative power, until it becomes turned back, as it were, upon itself, until the monad not only is a mirror, but knows itself as one, and you have man. The soul of man is the world come to consciousness of itself. The realm of monads in what we call the inorganic world and the lower organic realm shows us the monad let and hindered in its development. These realms attempt to speak forth the law of their being, and reveal the immanent presence of the universe; but they do not hear their own voice, their utterance is only for others. In man the universe is manifested, and is manifested to man himself.

CHAPTER IV.

LOCKE AND LEIBNIZ. — INNATE IDEAS.

THE reader, impatient of what may have seemed an over-long introduction, has perhaps been asking when he was to be brought to the subject under consideration, — the relations of Leibniz to Locke. But it has been impossible to come to this question until we had formed for ourselves an outline of the philosophical position of Leibniz. Nowhere in the "Nouveaux Essais" does Leibniz give a connected and detailed exposition of his philosophy, either as to his standpoint, his fundamental principles, or his method.

Some preliminary view of his position is therefore a necessity. The demand for this preliminary exposition becomes more urgent as we recognize that Leibniz's remarks upon Locke are not a critique of Locke from the standpoint of the latter, but are the application of his own philosophical conclusions. Criticism from within, an examination of a system of thought with relation to the consistency and coherency of its results, the connection between these results and the method professedly employed, investigation which depends not at all upon the position of the critic, but occupies itself with the internal relations of the system under discussion, — such criticism is a product of the present century. What we find in the "Nouveaux Essais" is a comparison of the ideas of Locke with those of Leibniz himself, a testing of the former by the latter as a standard, their acceptance when they conform, their rejection when they are opposed, their completion when they are in partial harmony.

The value of this sort of criticism is likely to be small and evanescent. If the system used as a standard is meagre and narrow, if it is without comprehensiveness and flexibility, it does not repay after-examination. The fact that the "Nouveaux Essais" of Leibniz have escaped the oblivion of the philosophical criticism of his day is proof, if proof still be needed, of the reasoned basis, the width of grasp, the fertility of suggestion which characterize the thought of Leibniz. But the fact that the criticism is, after all, external and not internal has made necessary the foregoing extended account of his method and general results.

On the other hand, what of Locke? How about him who is the recipient of the criticism? I assume that no extended account of his ideas is here necessary, and conceive myself to be justified in this assumption by the fact that we are already better acquainted with Locke. This acquaintance, indeed, is not confined to those who have expressly studied Locke. His thought is an inheritance into which every English-speaking person at least is born. Only he who does not think escapes this inheritance. Locke did the work which he had to do so thoroughly that every Englishman who will philosophize must either build upon Locke's foundations, or, with conscious purpose, clear the ground before building for himself. And it would be difficult to say that the acceptance of Locke's views would influence one's thought more than their rejection. This must not, of course, be taken too literally. It may be that one who is a lineal descendant of Locke in the spiritual generations of thought would not state a single important truth as Locke stated it, or that those who seek their method and results elsewhere have not repudiated the thought of Locke as expressly belonging to him.

But the fundamental principles of empiricism: its conception of intelligence as an individual possession; its idea of reality as something over against and distinct from mind; its explanation of knowledge as a process of action and reaction between these separate things; its account of our inability to know things as they really are, — these principles are congenital with our thinking. They are so natural that we either accept them as axiomatic, and accuse those who reject them of metaphysical subtlety, or, staggered perchance by some of their results, give them up with an effort. But it is an effort, and a severe one; and there is none of us who can tell when some remnant of the conception of intelligence as purely particular and finite will catch him tripping. On the other hand, we realize much better than those who have behind them a Leibniz and a Kant, rather than a Locke and a Hume, the meaning and the thorough-going necessity of the universality of intelligence. Idealism must be in some ways arbitrary and superficial to him who has not had a pretty complete course of empiricism.

Leibniz seems to have been impressed with the Essay on the Human Understanding at its first appearance. As early as 1696 we find him writing a few pages of comment upon the book. Compared with his later critique, these early "reflections" seem colorless, and give the impression that Leibniz desired to minimize his differences from Locke rather than to set them forth in relief. Comparatively slight as were his expressions of dissent, they appear to have stung Locke when they reached him. Meantime Locke's book was translated into French, and made its way to a wider circle of readers. This seems to have suggested to Leibniz the advisability of pursuing his comments somewhat further; and in the summer of 1703 he produced the work which now occupies us. A letter which Leibniz wrote at about this time is worth quoting at large for the light which it throws upon the man, as well as for suggesting the chief points in which he differed from Locke. Leibniz writes:—

"I have forgotten to tell you that my comments upon the work of Locke are nearly done. As he has spoken in a chapter of his second book about freedom, he has given me an opportunity to discuss that; and I hope that I may have done it in such a way as will please you. Above all, I have laid it upon myself to save the immateriality of the soul, which Locke leaves doubtful. I justify also the existence of innate ideas, and show that the soul produces their perception out of itself. Axioms, too, I approve, while Locke has a low opinion of them. In contradiction to him, I show that the individuality of man, through which he preserves his identity, consists in the duration of the simple or immaterial substance which animates him; that the soul is never without representations; that there is neither a vacuum nor atoms; that matter, or the passive principle, cannot be conscious, excepting as God unites with it a conscious substance. We disagree, indeed, in numerous other points, for I find that he rates too low the noble philosophy of the Platonic school (as Descartes did in part), and substitutes opinions which degrade us, and which may become hurtful to morals, though I am persuaded that Locke's intention was thoroughly good. I have made these comments in leisure hours, when I have been journeying or visiting, and could not occupy myself with investigations requiring great pains. The work has continued to grow under my hands, for in almost every chapter, and to a greater extent than I had thought possible, I have found matter for remark. You will be astonished when I tell you that I have worked upon this as upon something which requires no great pains. But the fact is, that I long ago established the general principles of philosophic subjects in my mind in a demonstrative way, or pretty nearly so, and that they do not require much new consideration from me."

Leibniz goes on to add that he has put these reflections in the form of a dialogue that they may be more attractive; has written them in the popular language, rather than in Latin, that they may reach as wide a circle as the work of Locke; and that he hopes to publish them soon, as Locke is already an old man, and he wishes to get them before the public while Locke may still reply.

But unfortunately this last hope was destined to remain unrealized. Before the work of revision was accomplished, Locke died. Leibniz, in a letter written in 1714, alludes to his controversy with Locke as follows: "I do not like the thought of publishing refutations of authors who are dead. These should appear during their life, and be communicated to them." Then, referring to his earlier comments, he says: "A few remarks escaped me, I hardly know how, and were taken to England. Mr. Locke, having seen them, spoke of them slightingly in a letter to Molineux. I am not astonished at it. We were somewhat too far apart in principle, and that which I suggested seemed paradoxical to him." Leibniz, according to his conviction here expressed, never published his "Nouveaux Essais sur l'Entendement Humain." Schaarschmidt remarks that another reason may have restrained him, in that he did not wish to carry on too many controversies at once with the English people. He had two on his hands then, — one with the Newtonians regarding the infinitesimal calculus; the other with Bishop Clarke regarding the nature of God, of time and space, of freedom, and cognate subjects. However, in 1765, almost fifty years after the death of Leibniz, his critique upon Locke finally appeared.

It is somewhat significant that one whose tendency was conciliatory, who was eminently what the Germans delight to call him, a "mediator," attempting to unite the varied truths which he found scattered in opposed systems, should have had so much of his work called forth by controversy. Aside from the cases just mentioned, his other chief work, the Theodicy, is, in form, a reply to Bayle. Many of his minor pieces are replies to criticism or are developments of his own thought with critical reference to Descartes, Malebranche, and others. But Leibniz has a somewhat different attitude towards his British and towards his Continental opponents. With the latter he was always in sympathy, while they in turn gave whatever he uttered a respectful hearing. Their mutual critiques begin and end in compliments. But the Englishmen found the thought of Leibniz "paradoxical" and forced. It seemed to them wildly speculative, and indeed arbitrary guess-work, without any special reason for its production, and wholly unverifiable in its results. Such has been the fate of much of the best German thought since that time in the land of the descendants of Newton and Locke. But Leibniz, on the other hand, felt as if he were dealing, in philosophical matters at least, with foemen hardly worthy of his steel. Locke, he says, had subtlety and address, and a sort of *superficial* metaphysics; but he was ignorant of the method of mathematics,—that is to say, from the standpoint of Leibniz, of the method of all science. We have already seen that he thought the examination of a work which had been the result of the continued labor of Locke was a matter for the leisure hours of his courtly visits. Indeed, he would undoubtedly have felt about it what he actually expressed regarding his controversy with Clarke,—that he engaged in it

> "Ludus et jocus, quia in philosophia
> Omnia percepi atque animo mecum ante peregi."

He regarded the English as superficial and without grasp of principles, as they thought him over-deep and over-theoretical.

From this knowledge of the external circumstances of the work of Leibniz and its relation to Locke, it is necessary that we turn to its internal content, to the thought of Leibniz as related to the ideas of Locke. The Essay on the Human Understanding is, as the name implies, an account of the nature of knowledge. Locke tells us that it originated in the fact that often, when he had been engaged in discussions with his friends, they found themselves landed in insoluble difficulties. This occurred so frequently that it seemed probable that they had been going at matters from the wrong side, and that before they attempted to come to conclusions about questions, they ought to examine the capacity of intelligence, and see whether it is fitted to deal with such questions. Locke, in a word, is another evidence of that truth which lies at the basis of all forms of philosophical thought, however opposed they may be to one another, — the truth that knowledge and reality are so organic to each other that to come to any conclusion about one, we must know something about the other. Reality equals objects known or knowable, and knowledge equals reality dissolved in ideas, — reality which has become translucent through its meaning.

Locke's Essay is, then, an account of the origin, nature, extent, and limitations of human knowledge. Such is its subject-matter. What is its method? Locke himself tells us that he uses the "plain historical method." We do not have to resort to the forcing of language to learn that this word "historical" contains the key to his work. Every page of the Essay is testimony to the fact that Locke always proceeds by inquiring into the way and circumstances by which knowledge of the subject under consideration came into existence and into the conditions by which it was developed. Origin means with Locke, not logical dependence, but temporal production; development means temporal succession. In the language of our day, Locke's Essay is an attempt to settle ontological questions by a psychological method. And as we have before noticed, Leibniz meets him, not by inquiry into the pertinence of the method or into the validity of results so reached, but by the more direct way of impugning his psychology, by substituting another theory of the nature of mind and of the way in which it works.

The questions with which the discussion begins are as to the existence of innate ideas, and as to whether the soul always thinks, — questions which upon their face will lead the experienced reader of to-day to heave a sigh in memory of hours wasted in barren dispute, and which will create a desire to turn elsewhere for matter more solid and more nutritive. But in this case, under the form which the discussion takes at the hands of Leibniz, the question which awaits answer under the meagre and worn-out formula of "innate ideas" is the function of intelligence in experience.

Locke denies, and denies with great vigor, the existence of innate ideas. His motives in so doing are practical and theoretical. He sees almost every old idea, every hereditary prejudice, every vested interest of thought, defended on the ground that it is an innate idea. Innate ideas were sacred, and everything which could find no defence before reason was an innate idea. Under such circumstances he takes as much interest in demolishing them as Bacon took in the destruction of the "eidols." But this is but a small portion of the object of Locke. He is a thorough-going empiricist; and the doctrine of innate ideas appears to offer the greatest obstacle to the acceptance of the truth that all the furnishing of the intellect comes from experience. Locke's metaphors for the mind are that it is a blank tablet, an empty closet, an unwritten book. The "innate idea" is only a sentence written by experience, but which, deified by a certain school of philosophers, has come to be regarded as eternally imprinted upon the soul.

Such, indeed, is Locke's understanding of the nature of innate ideas. He conceives of them as "characters *stamped*, as it were, upon the mind of man, which the soul has received in its first being and brings into the world with it;" or they are "constant *impressions* which the souls of men receive in their first beings." They are "truths *imprinted* upon the soul." Having this conception of what is meant by "innate ideas," Locke sets himself with great vigor, and, it must be confessed, with equal success, to their annihilation.

His argument is somewhat diffuse and scattered, but in substance it is as follows: Whatever is in the mind, the mind must be conscious of. "To be in the mind and not to be perceived, is all one as to say that anything is and is not in the mind." If there be anything in the mind which is innate, it must be present to the consciousness of all, and, it would seem, of all at all times, savages, infants, and idiots included. And as it requires little philosophical penetration to see that savages do not ponder upon the principle that whatever is, is; that infants do not dwell in their cradle upon the thought of contradiction, or idiots ruminate upon that of excluded middle, — it ought to be evident that such truths cannot be innate. Indeed, we must admit, with Locke, that probably few men ever come to the explicit consciousness of such ideas, and that these few are such as direct their minds to the matter with some pains. Locke's argument may be summed up in his words: If these are not notions naturally imprinted, how can they be innate? And if they are notions naturally imprinted, how can they be unknown?

But since it may be said that these truths are in the mind, but in such a way that it is only when they are proposed that men assent to them, Locke goes on to clinch his argument. If this be true, it shows that the ideas are not innate; for the same thing is true of a large number of scientific truths, those of mathematics and morals, as well as of purely sensible facts, as that red is not blue, sweet is not sour, etc.,—truths and facts which no one calls innate. Or if it be said that they are in the mind implicitly or potentially, Locke points out that this means either nothing at all, or else that the mind is *capable* of knowing them. If this is what is meant by innate ideas, then all ideas are innate; for certainly it cannot be denied that the mind is capable of knowing all that it ever does know, or, as Locke ingenuously remarks, "nobody ever denied that the mind was capable of knowing several truths."

It is evident that the force of Locke's contention against innate ideas rests upon a certain theory regarding the nature of innate ideas and of the relations of consciousness to intelligence. Besides this, there runs through his whole polemic the assertion that, after all, innate ideas are useless, as experience, in the sense of impressions received from without, and the formal action of intelligence upon them, is adequate to doing all they are supposed to do. It is hardly too much to say that the nerve of Locke's argument is rather in this positive assertion than in the negations which he brings against this existence. Leibniz takes issue with him on each of these three points. He has another conception of the very nature of innate ideas; he denies Locke's opinions about consciousness; he brings forward an opposed theory upon the relation of experience to reason. This last point we shall take up in a chapter by itself, as its importance extends far beyond the mere question as to the existence of ideas which may properly be called innate. The other two questions, as to the real character of innate ideas and the relation of an idea to consciousness, afford material to occupy us for the present.

The metaphor which Locke constantly uses is the clew to his conception of innate ideas. They are characters stamped or imprinted upon the mind, they exist *in* the mind. The mind would be just what it is, even if they had no existence. It would not have quite so much "in" it, but its own nature would not be changed. Innate ideas he conceives as bearing a purely external relation to mind. They are not organic to it, nor necessary instruments through which it expresses itself; they are mechanically impressed upon it. But what the "intellectual" school had meant by innate ideas was precisely that the relation of ideas to intelligence is *not* that of passive holding or containing on the side of mind, and of impressions or stamps on the side of the ideas. Locke reads the fundamental category of empiricism — mechanical relation, or external action — into the nature of innate ideas, and hence easily infers their absurdity. But the object of the upholders of innate ideas had been precisely to deny that this category was applicable to the whole of intelligence. By an innate idea they meant an assertion of the dynamic relation of intelligence and some of its ideas. They meant to assert that intelligence has a structure, which necessarily functions in certain ways. While Locke's highest conception of an innate idea was that it must be something ready made, dwelling in the mind prior to experience, Leibniz everywhere asserts that it is a connection and relation which forms the logical prius and the psychological basis of experience. He finds no difficulty in admitting all there is of positive truth in Locke's doctrine; namely, that we are not conscious of these innate ideas until a period later than that in which we are conscious of sensible facts, or, in many cases, are not conscious of them at all. This priority in time of sensible experience to rational knowledge, however, can become a reason for denying the "innate" character of the latter only when we suppose that they are two entirely different orders of fact, one knowledge due to experience, the other knowledge already formed and existing in the mind prior to "experience."

Leibniz's conception of the matter is brought out when he says that it is indeed true that we begin with particular experiences rather than with general principles, but that the order of nature is the reverse, for the ground, the basis of the particular truths is in the general; the former being in reality only instances of the latter. General principles, he says, enter into *all* our thoughts, and form their soul and interconnection. They are as necessary for thought as muscles and tendons are for walking, although we may not be conscious of their existence. This side of the teaching of Leibniz consists, accordingly, in the assertion that "innate" knowledge and knowledge derived from experience are not two kinds of knowledge, but rather two ways of considering it. If we consider it as it comes to us, piecemeal and fragmentary, a succession of particular instances, to be gathered up at a future time into general principles, and stated in a rational form, it is seen as empirical. But, after all, this is only a superficial and external way of looking at it. If we examine into it we shall see that there are contained in these transitory and particular experiences certain truths more general and fundamental, which condition them, and at the same time constitute their meaning.

If we inquire into the propriety of calling these truths "innate," we find it is because they are native to intelligence, and are not acquisitions which it makes. Indeed, it may be said that they *are* intelligence, so close and organic is their relation, just as the muscles, the tendons, the skeleton, are the body. Thus it is that Leibniz accepts the statement, *Nihil est in intellectu quod non fuerit in sensu*, with the addition of the statement *nisi ipse intellectus*. The doctrine of the existence of innate ideas is thus shown to mean that intelligence exists with a real content which counts for something in the realm of experience. If we take intelligence and examine into its structure and ascertain its modes of expression, we find organically inherent in its activity certain conceptions like unity, power, substance, identity, etc., and these we call "innate." An idea, in short, is no longer conceived as something existing in the mind or in consciousness; it is an activity of intelligence. An innate idea is a necessary activity of intelligence; that is, such an activity as enters into the framework of all experience.

Leibniz thus succeeds in avoiding two errors into which philosophers whose general aims are much like his have fallen. One is dividing *a priori* and *a posteriori* truths from each other by a hard and fixed line, so that we are conceived to have some knowledge which comes wholly from experience, while there is another which comes wholly from reason. According to Leibniz, there is no thought so abstract that it does not have its connection with a sensible experience, or rather its embodiment in it. And, on the other hand, there is no experience so thoroughly sensuous that it does not bear in itself traces of its origin in reason. "*All* our thoughts come from the depths of the soul," says Leibniz; there are none that "come" to us from without. The other error is the interpretation of the existence of innate ideas or "intuitions" (as this school generally calls them) in a purely formal sense. They are thus considered as truths contained in and somehow expressed by intelligence, but yet not so connected with it that in knowing them we necessarily know intelligence itself. They are considered rather as arbitrary determinations of truths by a power whose own nature is conceivably foreign to truth, than as so many special developments of an activity which may indifferently be called "intelligence" or "truth." Leibniz, however, never fails to state that an innate truth is, after all, but one form or aspect of the activity of the mind in knowing.

In this way, by bringing to light a deeper and richer conception of what in reality constitutes an innate idea, Leibniz answers Locke. His reply is indirect; it consists rather in throwing a flood of new light upon the matter discussed, than in a ponderous response and counter-attack. But when Leibniz touches upon the conception of a *tabula rasa*, of a mind which in itself is a mere blank, but has the capacity for knowing, he assumes the offensive. The idea of a bare capacity, a formal faculty, of power which does not already involve some actual content within itself, he repudiates as a relic of scholasticism. What is the soul, which has nothing until it gets it from without? The doctrine of a vacuum, an emptiness which is real, is always absurd;

and it is doubly so when to this vacuum is ascribed powers of feeling and thinking, as Locke does. Accepting for the moment the metaphor of a *tabula rasa*, Leibniz asks where we shall find a tablet which yet does not have some quality, and which is not a co-operating cause, at least, in whatever effects are produced upon it? The notion of a soul without thought, an empty tablet of the soul, he says, is one of a thousand fictions of philosophers. He compares it with the idea of "space empty of matter, absolute uniformity or homogeneity, perfect spheres of the second element produced by primordial perfect cubes, abstractions pure and simple, to which our ignorance and inattention give birth, but of which reality does not admit." If Locke admits then (as he does) certain capacities inherent in the soul, he cannot mean the scholastic fiction of bare capacity or mere possibility; he must mean "real possibilities,"—that is, capacities accompanied with some actual tendency, an inclination, a disposition, an aptitude, a preformation which determines our soul in a certain direction, and which makes it necessary that the possibility becomes actual. And this tendency, this actual inclination of intelligence in one way rather than another, so that it is not a matter of indifference to intelligence what it produces, is precisely what constitutes an innate idea. So Leibniz feels certain that at bottom Locke must agree with him in this matter if the latter is really in earnest in rejecting the "faculties" of the scholastics and in wishing for a real explanation of knowledge.

But the argument of Locke rests upon yet another basis. He founds his denial of innate ideas not only upon a static conception of their ready made existence "in" the soul, but also upon an equally mechanical conception of consciousness. "Nothing can be in the mind which is not in consciousness." This statement appears axiomatic to Locke, and by it he would settle the whole discussion. Regarding it, Leibniz remarks that if Locke has such a prejudice as this, it is not surprising that he rejects innate ideas. But consciousness and mental activity are not thus identical. To go no farther, the mere empirical fact of memory is sufficient to show the falsity of such an idea. Memory reveals that we have an indefinite amount of knowledge of which we are not always conscious. Rather than that knowledge and consciousness are one, it is true that actual consciousness only lays hold of an infinitesimal fraction of knowledge. But Leibniz does not rely upon the fact of memory alone. We must constantly keep in mind that to Leibniz the soul is not a form of being wholly separate from nature, but is the culmination of the system of reality. The reality is everywhere the monad, and the soul is the monad with the power of feeling, remembering, and connecting its ideas. The activities of the monad, those representative changes which sum up and symbolize the universe, do not cease when we reach the soul. They are continued. If the soul has the power of attention, they are potentially conscious. Such as the soul actually attends to, thus giving them relief and making them distinct, are actually conscious. But all of them exist.

Thus it is that Leibniz not only denies the equivalence of soul and consciousness, but asserts that the fundamental error of the psychology of the Cartesians (and here, at least, Locke is a Cartesian) is in identifying them. He asserts that "unconscious ideas" are of as great importance in psychology as molecules are in physics. They are the link between unconscious nature and the conscious soul. Nothing happens all at once; nature never makes jumps; these facts stated in the law of continuity necessitate the existence of activities, which may be called ideas, since they belong to the soul and yet are not in consciousness.

When, therefore, Locke asks how an innate idea can exist and the soul not be conscious of it, the answer is at hand. The "innate idea" exists as an activity of the soul by which it represents — that is, expresses — some relation of the universe, although we have not yet become conscious of what is contained or enveloped in this activity. To become conscious of the innate idea is to lift it from the sphere of nature to the conscious life of spirit. And thus it is, again, that Leibniz can assert that all ideas whatever proceed from the depths of the soul. It is because it is the very being of the soul as a monad to reflect "from its point of view" the world. In this way Leibniz brings the discussion regarding innate ideas out of the plane of examination into a matter of psychological fact into a consideration of the essential nature of spirit. An innate idea is now seen to be one of the relations by which the soul reproduces some relation which constitutes the universe of reality, and at the same time realizes its own individual nature. It is one reflection from that spiritual mirror, the soul. With this enlarged and transformed conception of an idea apt to be so meagre we may well leave the discussion. There has been one mind at least to which the phrase "innate ideas" meant something worth contending for, because it meant something real.

CHAPTER V.

SENSATION AND EXPERIENCE.

A CAREFUL study of the various theories which have been held concerning sensation would be of as much interest and importance as an investigation of any one point in the range of philosophy. In the theory of a philosopher about sensation we have the reflex of his fundamental category and the clew to his further doctrine. Sensation stands on the border-line between the world of nature and the realm of soul, and every advance in science, every development of philosophy, leaves its impress in a change in the theory of sensation. Apparently one of the simplest and most superficial of questions, in reality it is one of the most difficult and far-reaching. At first sight it seems as if it were a sufficient account of sensation to say that an object affects the organ of sense, and thus impresses upon the mind the quality which it possesses. But this simple statement arouses a throng of further questions: How is it possible that one substance, — matter, — should affect another, — mind? How can a causal relation exist between them? Is the mind passive or active in this impression? How can an object convey unchanged to the mind a quality which it possesses?

Or is the sensational *quale* itself a product of the mind's activity? If so, what is the nature of the object which excites the sensation? As known, it is only a collection of sensuous qualities; if these are purely mental, what becomes of the object? And if there is no object really there, what is it that excites the sensation? Such questionings might be continued almost indefinitely; but those given are enough to show that an examination of the nature and origin of sensation introduces us to the problems of the relation of intelligence and the world; to the problem of the ultimate constitution of an object which is set over against a subject and which affects it; and to the problem of the nature of mind, which as thus affected from without must be limited in its nature, but which as bearer of the whole known universe must be in some sense infinite. If we consider, not the mode of production of sensation, but its relation to knowledge, we find philosophical schools divided into two, — Sensationalists, and Rationalists. If we inquire into its functions, we find that the empiricist sees in it convincing evidence of the fact that all knowledge originates from a source *extra mentem;* that the intellectual idealist finds in it evidence of the gradual transition of nature into spirit; that the ethical idealist, like Kant and Fichte, sees in it the material of the phenomenal world, which is necessary in its opposition to the rational sphere in order that there may occur that conflict of pure law and sensuous impulse which alone makes morality possible. We thus realize that as we look at the various aspects of sensation, we are taken into the discussion of ontology, of the theory of knowledge and of ethics.

Locke virtually recognizes the extreme importance of the doctrine of sensation, and his second book might almost be entitled "Concerning the Nature and Products of Sensation." On the other hand, one of the most characteristic and valuable portions of the reply of Leibniz is in his development of a theory of sensation which is thoroughly new, except as we seek for its germs in its thoughts of Plato and Aristotle. According to Locke, knowledge originates from two sources, — sensation and reflection. Sensations are "the impressions made on our senses by outward objects that are extrinsic to the mind." When the mind "comes to reflect on its own operations about the ideas got by sensation, and thereby stores itself with a new set of ideas," it gets ideas of reflection.

If we leave out of account for the present the ideas of reflection, we find that the ideas which come through sensation have two main characteristics. First, in having sensations, the mind is passive; its part is purely receptive. The objects impress themselves upon the mind, they obtrude into consciousness, whether the mind will or not. There is a purely external relation existing between sensation and the understanding. The ideas are offered to the mind, and the understanding cannot refuse to have them, cannot change them, blot them out, nor create them, any more than a mirror can refuse, alter, or obliterate the images which objects produce in it. Sensation, in short, is a purely passive having of ideas. Secondly, every sensation is simple. Locke would say of sensations what Hume said of all ideas, — every distinct sensation is a separate existence. Every sensation is "uncompounded, containing nothing but one uniform appearance, not being distinguishable into different ideas." Knowledge is henceforth a process of compounding, of repeating, comparing, and uniting sensation. Man's understanding "reaches no further than to compound and divide the materials that are made to his hand."

It hardly need be said that Locke has great difficulty in keeping up this thoroughly atomic theory of mind. It is a theory which makes all relations external; they are, as Locke afterwards says, "superinduced" upon the facts. It makes it impossible to account for any appearance of unity and connection among ideas, and Locke quietly, and without any consciousness of the contradiction involved, introduces certain inherent relations into the structure of the ideas when he comes to his constructive work. "Existence and unity are two ideas," he says, "that are suggested to the understanding by every object without, and every idea within."

At other places he introduces the idea of quality of a substance, effect of a cause, continued permanence or identity into a sensation, as necessary constituents of it; thus making a sensation a unity of complex elements instead of an isolated bare notion. How far he could have got on in his account of knowledge without this surreptitious qualifying of a professedly simple existence, may be seen by asking what would be the nature of a sensation which did not possess existence and unity, and which was not conceived as the quality of a thing or as the effect of an external reality.

This digression has been introduced at this point because the next character of a sensation which Locke discusses is its objective character, — its relation to the object which produces it. To discourse of our ideas intelligibly, he says, it will be convenient to distinguish them as they are ideas in our minds and as they are modifications of matter in the bodies that cause them. In other words, he gives up all thought of considering ideas as simply mental modifications, and finds it necessary to take them in their relations to objects.

Taking them in this way, he finds that they are to be divided into two classes, of which one contains those ideas that are copies and resemblances of qualities in the objects, ideas "which are really in the object, whether we take notice of them or no," — in which case we have an idea of the thing as it is in itself; while the other class contains those which are in no way resemblances of the objects which produce them, "having no more similitude than the idea of pain and of a sword." The former are primary qualities, and are solidity, extension, figure, motion or rest, and number; while the secondary qualities are colors, smells, and tastes. The former ideas are produced by impulse of the bodies themselves, which simply effect a transference of their qualities over into the mind; while the secondary qualities are arbitrarily annexed by the power of God to the objects which excite them.

It will be noticed that there are two elements which make the sensation of Locke what it is. With reference to its *production*, it is the effect which one substance, matter, has upon another substance, mind, which is unlike it in nature, and between which whatever relations exist, are thoroughly incomprehensible, so that, indeed, their connections with each other can be understood only by recourse to a *tertium quid*, an omnipotent power which can arbitrarily produce such collocations as please it. With reference to its *function*, it is the isolated and "simple" (that is, non-relational) element out of which all actual forms of knowledge are made by composition and re-arrangement.

Leibniz, without entering into explicit criticism of just these two points, develops his own theory with reference to them. To Leibniz, reality constitutes a system; that is, it is of such a nature that its various portions have an essential and not merely external relation to one another. Sensation is of course no exception. It is not a mere accident, nor yet a supernatural yoking of things naturally opposed. It has a meaning in that connection of things which constitute the universe. It contributes to the significance of the world. It is one way in which those activities which make the real express themselves. It has its place or reason in the totality of things, and this whether we consider its origin or its position with regard to knowledge. In a word, while the characteristic of Locke's theory is that he conceives sensation as in external relation both to reality, as mechanically produced by it, and to knowledge, as being merely one of the atomic elements which may enter into a compound, Leibniz regards reality as organic to sensation, and this in turn as organic to knowledge. We have here simply an illustration of the statement with which we set out; namely, that the treatment of sensation always reflects the fundamental philosophical category of the philosopher.

All reality exists in the form of monads; monads are simple substances whose nature is action; this action consists in representing, according to a certain law of succession, the universe. Various monads have various degrees of activity; that is, of the power of reflecting the world. So much of Leibniz's general philosophical attitude it is necessary to recall, to understand what he means by "sensation." The generic name which is applied to this mirroring activity of the monads is "perception," which, as Leibniz often says, is to be carefully distinguished from apperception, which is the representation become conscious. Perception may be defined, therefore, as the inclusion of the many or multiform (the world of objects) in a unity (the simple substance). It was the great defect of previous philosophy that it "considered only spirits or self-conscious beings as souls," and had consequently recognized only conscious perceptions. It had been obliged, therefore, to make an impassable gulf between mind and matter, and sensations were thus rendered inexplicable. But Leibniz finds his function as a philosopher in showing that these problems, which seem insoluble, arise when we insist upon erecting into actual separations or differences of kind what really are only stages of development or differences of degree. A sensation is not an effect which one substance impresses upon another because God pleased that it should, or because of an incomprehensible incident in the original constitution of things. It is a higher development of that representative power which belongs to every real being.

Certain monads reach a state of development, or manifestation of activity, which is characterized by the possession of distinct organs. Such monads may be called, in a pre-eminent sense, "souls," and include all the higher animals as well as man. This possession of differentiated organs finds its analogue in the internal condition of the monad. What appears externally as an organ of sense appears ideally as a conscious representative state which we call "sensation." "When," Leibniz says, "the monad has its organs so developed that there is relief and differentiation in the impressions received, and consequently in the perceptions which represent them, we have feeling or sensation; that is, a perception accompanied by memory," to which at other times he adds "attention." Life, he says, "is a perceptive principle; the soul is sensitive life; mind is rational soul." And again he says in substance that when the soul begins to have interests, and to regard one representation as of more value than others, it introduces relief into its perceptions, and those which stand out are called "sensations."

This origin of sensations as higher developments of the representative activities of a monad conditions their relation to further processes of knowledge. The sensations are confused knowledge; they are ideas in their primitive and most undifferentiated form. They constitute, as Leibniz somewhere says, the vertigo of the conscious life. In every sentient organism multitudes of sensations are constantly thronging in and overpowering its distinct consciousness. The soul is so flooded with ideas of everything in the world which has any relation to its body that it has distinct ideas of nothing. Higher knowledge, then, does not consist in compounding these sensations; that would literally make confusion worse confounded. It consists in introducing distinctness into the previously confused sensations,—in finding out what they mean; that is, in finding out their bearings, what they point to, and how they are related. Knowledge is not an external process performed upon the sensations, it is the development of their internal content.

It follows, therefore, that sensation is organic to all forms of knowledge whatever. The monad, which is pure activity, that which culminates the scale of reality, has no confused ideas, and to it all knowledge is eternally rational, having no sensible traces about it. But every other monad, having its activity limited, has ideas which come to it at first in a confused way, and which its activity afterwards differentiates. Thus it is that Leibniz can agree so heartily with the motto of the Sensationalist school, — that there is nothing in the intellect which was not first in the sensory. But Leibniz uses this phrase as Aristotle would have done, having in mind the distinction between potentiality and actuality. *In posse*, sensation is all knowledge; but only *in posse*. And he, like Aristotle, interprets the relation between potentiality and actuality as one of a difference of activity. The potential is that which becomes real through a dynamic process. The actual is capacity plus action. Sensation, in short, is spiritual activity in an undeveloped and hence partial and limited condition. It is not, as Locke would have it, the real factor in all knowledge.

The marks of sensation which Locke lays down, — their passivity, their simplicity, their position as the real element in knowledge, — Leibniz either denies, therefore, or accepts in a sense different from that of Locke. Strictly speaking, sensation is an activity of the mind. There are no windows through which the soul receives impressions. Pure passivity of any kind is a myth, as scholastic fiction. Sensation is developed from the soul within; it is the activity of reality made manifest to itself. It is a higher kind of action than anything we find in minerals or in plants. If we look at sensation ideally, however, that is, according to the position which it holds in the system of knowledge, it is properly regarded as passive. It represents the limitation, the unrealized (that is, the non-active) side of spiritual life.

"Efficient causality" is a term which has its rightful and legitimate use in physical science. Simply from the scientific point of view we are correct in speaking of objects as affecting the body, and the body, through its nervous system, as affecting the soul and producing sensations. But philosophy does not merely use categories, it explains them. And Leibniz contends that to explain the category of causality in a mechanical sense, to understand by it physical influence actually transferred from one thing to another, is to make the idea inexplicable and irrational. The true meaning of causality is ideal. It signifies the relative positions which the objects concerned have in the harmonious system of reality. The body that is higher in the scale impresses the other; that is to say, it dominates it or gives its law. There is no energy or quality which passes physically from one to the other. But one monad, as higher in the stage of development than another, makes an ideal demand upon that one. It places before the other its own more real condition. The less-developed monad, since its whole activity consists in representing the universe of reality, answers to this demand by developing the corresponding quality in itself. The category of harmonious or co-operative action is thus substituted for that of external and mechanical influence. Physical causality when given a philosophic interpretation means organic development. The reality of a higher stage is the more active: the more active has a greater content in that it mirrors the universe more fully; it manifests accordingly more of the law of the universe, and hence has an ideal domination over that which is lower in the scale. It is actually (that is, in activity) what the other is potentially. But as the entire existence of the latter is in representing or setting forth the relations which make the world, its activity is aroused to a corresponding production. Hence the former is called "cause," and the latter "effect."

This introduces us to the relation of soul and body, or, more generally stated, to the relation of mind and matter. It is the theory of co-operation, of harmonious activity, which Leibniz substitutes for the theory which Descartes had formulated, according to which there are two opposed substances which can affect each other only through the medium of a *deus ex machina*. Locke, on the other hand, took the Cartesian principle for granted, and thus enveloped himself in all the difficulties which surround the question of "mind and matter." Locke wavers between two positions, one of which is that there are two unknown substances, — the soul and the object in itself, — which, coming in contact, produce sensations; while the other takes the hypothetical attitude that there may be but one substance, — matter, — and that God, out of the plenitude of his omnipotence, has given matter a capacity which does not naturally belong to it, — that of producing sensations. In either case, however, the final recourse is to the arbitrary power of God. There is no natural — that is, intrinsic and explicable — connection between the sensation and that which produces it. Sensation occupied the hard position which the mechanical school of to-day still allots it. It is that "inexplicable," "mysterious," "unaccountable" link between the domains of matter and mind of which no rational account can be given, but which is yet the source of all that we know about matter, and the basis of all that is real in the mind!

Leibniz, recognizing that reality is an organic whole, — not two parts with a chasm between them, — says that "God does not arbitrarily give substances whatever qualities may happen, or that he may arbitrarily determine, but only such as are natural; that is, such as are related to one another in an *explicable* way as modifications of the substance." Leibniz feels sure that to introduce the idea of the inexplicable, the purely supernatural, into the natural is to give up all the advantages which the modern mechanical theory had introduced, and to relapse into the meaningless features of scholasticism. If the "supernatural" — that is, the essentially inexplicable — is introduced in this one case, why should it not be in others; why should we not return outright to the "fanatic philosophy which explains all facts by simply attributing them to God immediately or by way of miracle, or to the barbarian philosophy, which explains phenomena by manufacturing, *ad hoc*, occult qualities or faculties, seemingly like little demons or spirits capable of performing, without ceremony, whatever is required, — as if watches marked time by their horodeictic power, without wheels, and mills ground grain, without grindstones, by their fractive power"? In fact, says Leibniz, by introducing the inexplicable into our *explanations* "we fall into something worse than occult qualities, — we give up philosophy and reason; we open asylums for ignorance and laziness, holding not only that there are qualities which we do not understand (there are, indeed, too many such), but qualities which the greatest intelligence, if God gave it all the insight possible, could not understand, — that is, such as are *in themselves* without rhyme or reason. And indeed it would be a thing without rhyme or reason that God should perform miracles in the ordinary course of nature." And regarding the whole matter of introducing the inconceivable and the inexplicable into science, he says that "while the conception of men is not the measure of God's power, their capacity of conception is the measure of *nature's* power, since everything occurring in the natural order is capable of being understood by the created intelligence." Such being the thought of Leibniz regarding the virtual attempt to introduce in his day the unknowable into philosophy, it is evident that he must reject, from the root up, all theories of sensation which, like Locke's, make it the product of the inexplicable intercourse of two substances.

For this doctrine, then, Leibniz substitutes that of an infinite number of substances, all of the same kind, all active, all developing from within, all conspiring to the same end, but of various stages of activity, or bearing various relations of completeness to the one end.

Indeed, one and the same monad has various degrees of activity in itself; that is, it represents more or less distinctly the universe according to its point of view. Its point of view requires of it, of course, primarily, a representation of that which is about it. Thus an infinity of states arises, each corresponding to some one of the multitude of objects surrounding the monad. The soul has no control, no mastery, over these states. It has to take them as they come; with regard to them, the soul appears passive. It appears so because it does not as yet clearly distinguish them. It does not react upon them and become conscious of their meaning or thoroughly rational character. We shall afterwards see that "matter" is, with Leibniz, simply this passive or confused side of monads. It is the monad so far as it has not brought to light the rational activity which is immanent in it. At present we need only notice that the body is simply the part of matter or of passivity which limits the complete activity of any monad. So Leibniz says, "in so far as the soul has perfection, it has distinct thoughts, and God has accommodated the body to the soul. So far as it is imperfect and its perceptions are confused, God has accommodated the soul to the body in such a way that the soul lets itself be inclined by the passions, which are born from corporeal representations. It is by its confused thoughts (sensations) that the soul represents the bodies about it," just as, we may add, its distinct thoughts represent the monads or souls about it, and, in the degree of their distinctness, God, the monad which is *purus actus*.

Following the matter into more detail, we may say that since God alone is pure energy, knowing no limitation, God alone is pure spirit. Every finite soul is joined to an organic body. "I do not admit," says Leibniz, "that there are souls entirely separate from matter, nor created spirits detached from body. . . . It is this body which the monad represents most distinctly; but since this body expresses the entire universe by the connection of all matter throughout it, the soul represents the entire universe in representing the body which belongs to it most particularly." But according to the principle of continuity there must be in the least apparent portion of matter still "a universe of creatures, of souls, of entelechies. There is nothing sterile, nothing dead in the universe. It is evident from these considerations that every living body has a dominant entelechy, which is the soul in that body, but that the members of this living body are again full of other living beings and souls," which, however, since not of so high a grade, that is, not representing the universe so fully, appear to be wholly material and subject to the "dominant" entelechy; namely, to the one which gives the law to the others by expressing more adequately the idea at which they only confusedly aim. Owing to the constant change of activity, however, these particles do not remain in constant subordination to the same entelechy (that is, do not form parts of the same body), but pass on to higher or lower degrees of "evolution," and have their places taken by others undergoing similar processes of change. Thus "all bodies are in a perpetual flux, like rivers, with parts continually leaving and entering in." Or, interpreting this figurative language, each monad is continually, in its process of development, giving law to new and less developed monads, which therefore appear as its body. The nature of matter in itself, and of its phenomenal manifestation in the body, are, however, subjects which find no explanation here, and which will demand explanation in another chapter.

We may sum up Leibniz's theory of sensation by saying that it is a representative state developed by the self-activity of the soul; that in itself it is a confused or "involved" grade of activity, and in its relation to the world represents the confused or passive aspects of existence; that this limitation of the monad constitutes matter, and in its necessary connection with the monad constitutes the body which is always joined to the finite soul; that to this body are joined in all cases an immense number of monads, whose action is subordinate to that of this dominant monad, and that it is the collection of these which constitute the visible animal body. Thus if we look at sensation with regard to the monad which possesses it, it is a product of the body of the monad; if we look at it with reference to other monads, it represents or reflects their passive or material side. This is evidently one aspect again of the pre-established harmony, — an aspect in which some of the narrower of Leibniz's critics have seen the whole meaning of the doctrine exhausted. It is, however, simply one of the many forms in which the harmony, the union of spiritual and mechanical, ideal and material, meets us. In truth, while in other systems the fact of sensation is a fact demanding some artificial mode of reconciling "mind" and "matter," or is else to be accepted as an inexplicable fact, in the system of Leibniz it is itself evidence that the spiritual and the mechanical are not two opposed kinds of existence, but are organically united. It is itself the manifestation of the harmony of the ideal and the material, not something which requires that a factitious theory be invented for explaining their appearance of harmony. Sensation has within itself the ideal element, for it is the manifestation, in its most undeveloped form, of the spiritual meaning of the universe. It has a mechanical element, for it expresses the limitation, the passivity, of the monad.

It is from this standpoint that Leibniz criticises what Locke says about the relation of sensations to the objects which produce them. Leibniz holds that all our sensations have a definite and natural connection with the qualities of objects, — the "secondary" as well as the "primary." They all represent certain properties of the object. Even the pain which the thrust of a needle gives us, while it does not resemble anything in the needle, does in some way represent or resemble motions going on in our body. This resemblance is not necessarily one of exact form, but just as the ellipse, hyperbola, and parabola are projections of the circle in the sense that there is a natural and fixed law of connection between them, so that every point of one corresponds by a certain relation with every point of the other, so the resemblance between the sensation and the quality of the object is always in the form of a fixed law of order, which, however unknown to us it may now be, is capable of being found out. If we are to make any distinction between "secondary" and "primary" sensations, it should be not that one presents qualities that are in the objects, and the other affections which exist only in us, but that the primary sensations (of number, form, size, etc.) represent the qualities in a distinct way, appealing to the rational activity of intelligence, while the secondary represent the qualities in a confused way, a way not going beyond the effect upon the mind into relations, that is, into distinct knowledge.

This brings regularly before us the question of the relation of sensations to knowledge. We have seen enough already to know that Leibniz does not believe that knowledge begins with the simple (that is, unrelated), and then proceeds by a process of compounding. The sensation is not simple to Leibniz, but thoroughly complex, involving confusedly within itself all possible relations. As relations are brought forth into distinct light out of this confusion, knowledge ends rather than begins with the simple. And again it is evident that Leibniz cannot believe that knowledge begins and ends in experience, in the sense in which both himself and Locke use the word; namely, as meaning the combination and succession of impressions.

"Experience," as they use the term, consists in sensations and their association, — "consecution" as Leibniz calls it. Experience is the stage of knowledge reached by animals, and in which the majority of men remain, — and indeed all men in the greater part of their knowledge. Leibniz takes just the same position regarding the larger part of our knowledge which Hume takes regarding it all. It consists simply in associations of such a nature that when one part recurs there is a tendency to expect the recurrence of the other member. It resembles reason, but it is based on the accidental experience of events in a consecutive order, and not on knowledge of their causal connection. We all expect the sun to rise to-morrow; but with all of us, excepting the astronomer, such expectation is purely "empirical," being based on the images of past experiences which recur. The astronomer, however, sees into the grounds, that is, the reasons, of the expectation, and hence his knowledge is rational.

Thus we have two grades of knowledge, — one empirical, consisting of knowledge of facts; the other rational, being of the truths of reason. The former is contingent and particular, the latter is necessary and universal. Leibniz insists, with a pertinacity which reminds us of Kant, that "experience" can give instances or examples only, and that the fact that anything has happened in a given way any number of times in the past, can give no assurance that it will continue to do so in the future. There is nothing in the nature of the case which renders its exact opposite impossible. But a rational truth is necessary, for its opposite is impossible, being irrational or meaningless. This may not always be evident in the case of a complex rational truth; but if it be analyzed into simpler elements, as a geometrical proposition into definitions, axioms, and postulates, the absurdity of its opposite becomes evident. Sensation, in conclusion, is the having of confused ideas, — ideas corresponding to matter. Experience is the association of these confused ideas, and their association according to their accidental juxtaposition in the life of the soul. It therefore is not only thoroughly sensible, but is also phenomenal. Its content is sensations; its form is contingent and particular consecution. Both form and content, accordingly, need to be reconstructed if they are to be worthy of the name of science or of knowledge. This is the position which Leibniz assumes as against the empiricist, Locke. The details of this reconstruction, its method and result, we must leave till we come in the course of the argument again to the subject of knowledge.

CHAPTER VI.

THE IMPULSES AND THE WILL.

LOCKE, after discussing the subject of innate ideas in their relation to knowledge, goes on to discuss their practical side, or connection with will. We shall follow him in this as Leibniz does; but we shall consider in connection with this, Leibniz's general theory of will, which is developed partially in this chapter, but more completely in his critical remarks upon what Locke has to say of the notion of "power." Since the theory of morals is as closely connected with will as the theory of knowledge is with the intellect, we shall supplement this discussion with what Leibniz says upon the ethical question, drawing our material somewhat freely from his other writings.

The doctrine of will which Leibniz propounds is in closest harmony with his conception of intelligence, and this not merely in the way of empirical juxtaposition, but as the result of his fundamental principles. If we recall what has been said concerning the monad, we shall remember that it is an activity, but an activity with a content. It is a force, but a force which mirrors the universe. The content, that portion of reality which is reflected in the action, is knowledge, or the idea; the activity which brings this about is will, or the volition. They are related to each other as form and content. There is, strictly speaking, no "state" of mind; there is only a tension, a pushing forward of mind. There is no idea which is not a volition. Will is thus used, in a very broad sense, as equivalent to action. Since, however, the activity of the monad is in no case aimless, but has an end in view, the will is not *mere* activity in general, it is action towards some definite end. And since the end at which the monad aims is always the development of an idea, the reflection of some constituent of the universe, the will is always directed towards and determined by some idea of the intellect.

We have seen, however, that there are various stages in the reflecting power of the soul, or in the realization of intellect. Taking only the broadest division, there are perception and apperception; that is, there are the conscious and the unconscious mirroring of reality. We shall expect, then, to find two corresponding stages of volition. Leibniz calls these stages "appetition" and "volition" in the narrower sense. The constant tendency in every monad to go from one perception to another, — that is, the following of the law of development, — constitutes appetition. If joined to feeling, it constitutes instinct. Since, again, there are two degrees of apperception, one of empirical, the other of rational, consciousness, we shall expect to find two grades of volition proper, — one corresponding to action for conscious particular ends; the other for ends which are proposed by reason, and are hence universal. In this chapter we shall simply expand and illustrate these various propositions.

Sensations, looked at not as to what they represent, but in themselves, are impulses. As such they constitute the lowest stage of will. Impulsive action then includes all such as occurs for an end which is unknown, or at best but dimly felt. Such action may be called blind, not in the sense that it is without reason, but in the sense that reason is not consciously present. We are not to think of this instinctive action, however, as if it were found simply in the animals. Much of human action is also impulsive; probably, indeed, an impulsive factor is contained in our most rational willing. We are never able to take complete account of the agencies which are acting upon us. Along with the reasons of which we are conscious in choosing, there are mingled faint memories of past experience, subconscious solicitations of the present, dim expectations for the future. Such elements are decisive factors far more than we realize.

Indeed, it is because of the extent to which such unconscious influences bear upon us and move us that there arises the idea of indifferent or unmotivated choice. Were both motive and choice unconscious, the question as to whether choice were antecedently determined would not arise; and were our motives and their results wholly in consciousness, the solution of the question would be evident. But when we are conscious of our choice, but are not conscious of our impulses and motives, we get the impression that our choice is unmotived, and hence come to believe in "indifferent freedom," — the ability to choose as we will.

We shall shortly take up in more detail the theory of Leibniz regarding the freedom of will; and it is needful here to remark only that the conception which makes it consist in ability to choose without reason is in direct contradiction to his fundamental thought, — namely, that there can be no activity which does not aim at some reflection of the universe, by which, therefore, it is determined. From the psychological point of view, it is interesting also to notice how Leibniz's theory of unconscious ideas enables him to dispose of the strongest argument for indifferent choice, — that drawn from the immediate "testimony" of consciousness.

Upon the origin and nature of desires Leibniz has much more to say than about the impulses. His account of the transition from impulse to desire is based upon the conception of unconscious ideas. Slight and imperceptible impulses are working upon us all the time. Indeed, they are a necessity; for the actual state of a soul or monad at any time is, of course, one of incompleteness. Our nature must always work to free itself from its hindrances and obtain its goal of complete development. But it will not do this unless there is some stimulus, some solicitation to induce it to overcome its limitation. There is found accordingly in our every condition a feeling of dissatisfaction, or, using Locke's word, of "uneasiness;" and it is this which calls forth that activity which brings about a nearer approach to the soul's real good. But Leibniz differs from Locke in saying that this feeling of uneasiness is not a distinct, or even in most cases a conscious, one. It is not pain, although it differs from pain only in degree. Uneasiness and pain are related to each other as appetite for food is to hunger, — the first suffices to stimulate us to satisfaction, but if the want is not met, results in actual pain; if met, these "half pains" become tributary to pleasure itself. These unconscious stimuli to action result in actions which meet the want, and the aggregation of these satisfactions results in pleasure. In Leibniz's own words: —

"If these elements of pain were themselves true pains, we should always be in a state of misery, even in pursuing the good. But since there is always going on a summation of minute successes in overcoming these states of uneasiness, and these put us more and more at ease, there comes about a decided pleasure, which often has greater value even than the enjoyment of the good. Far, then, from regarding this uneasiness as a thing incompatible with happiness, I find that it is an essential condition of our happiness. For this does not consist in perfect possession, which would make us insensible and stupid, but in a constant progress towards greater results, which must always be accompanied, accordingly, by this element of desire or uneasiness."

And again he says that "we enjoy all the advantages of pain without any of its inconveniences. If the uneasiness should become too distinct, we should be miserable in our awaiting the good which relieves it; but as it is, there is a constant victory over these half-pains, which we always find in desire, and this gives us a quantity of half-pleasures, whose continuance and summation (for they acquire force like a moving body as it falls) result in a whole and true pleasure." In short, there is indeed an element of pain in all desire which stimulates us to action, and therefore to higher development. But ordinarily this element of pain is not present as such in consciousness, but is absorbed in the pleasure which accompanies the realization of the higher good. Thus Leibniz, accepting and emphasizing the very same fact that served Schopenhauer as a psycho-logical base of pessimism, uses it as a foundation-stone of optimism.

But desire, or the conscious tendency towards something required as a good, accompanied by the dim feeling of uneasiness at its absence, does not yet constitute the complete act of volition. "Several impulses and inclinations meet in forming the complete volition which is the result of their conflict." In the concrete act of will there are contained impulses which push us towards some end whose nature is not known; there is desire both in its inchoate stage, where pleasure and pain are not in consciousness, and in its formed state, where the pain and pleasure are definitely presented. Mixed with these desires and impulses are images of past experiences which call up the feelings which were formerly attached to them, and thus there are aroused indirectly additional impulses and desires. Out of this complicated mass of impulses, desires, and feelings, both original and reproduced, comes the "dominant effort" which constitutes complete will. But what governs the production of this prevailing or dominant effort, which we may interpret as the act of choice? The answer is simple: the result of the conflict of these various factors, the striking of the balance, *is* the choice. Some desire emerges from the confused complex, and that desire is the final determination of the will. This desire may not in all cases be the strongest in itself, — that is, the one whose satisfaction will allay the greatest "uneasiness," for the others, taken together, may outweigh it; it may, so to speak, have a plurality, but not a majority, of volitional forces on its side, — and in this case a fusion of opposing factors may defeat it. But in any event the result will be the *algebraic* sum of the various desires and impulses.

It is not at all necessary, however, that the net outcome shall make itself apparent as a mechanical equivalent of the forces at work. The soul, Leibniz says, may use its skill in the formation of parties, so as to make this or that side the victor. How is this to be done, and still disallow the possibility of arbitrary choice? This problem is solved through action becoming deliberate. Deliberate action is impossible unless the soul has formed the habit of looking ahead and of arranging for modes of action which do not present themselves as immediate necessities. Only in this way can one look at the matter impartially and coolly; "at the moment of combat there is no time for discussion. Everything which then occurs throws its full force on the balance, and contributes to an outcome made up in the same way as in mechanics." The formation of certain habits beforehand, therefore, is the secret of translating impulsive action into the deliberate sphere.

Of these habits the simplest consists in thinking only occasionally and incidentally of certain things. Imagination is the mother of desire. If we do not allow the imagination to dwell upon certain lines of thought, the probability of such thoughts acquiring sufficient force to become motives of weight is small. A still more effective method of regulating action is "to accustom ourselves to forming a train of thoughts of which reason, and not chance (that is, association), is the basis. We must get out of the tumult of present impressions, beyond our immediate surroundings, and ask: *Dic cur hic? respice finem!*" In other words, we must cross-question our impulses and desires, we must ask whence they come, that we may see how valid are the credentials which they offer. We must ask whither they tend, that we may measure them, not by their immediate interest, but by their relation to an end. The desires are not to be taken at their face-value, but are to be weighed and compared.

Such a process will evidently result in arresting

instantaneous action. There will be a pause between the presentation of the desires and the overt act. During this pause it may well occur that the examination to which the desires have been subject has awakened contrary desires. The thought of the ignoble origin of a desire or of its repulsive, though remote, result will bring into action desires of an opposed kind. Thus the soul regulates action, not as if, however, it had any direct influence over desires, but by its ability of bringing other desires into the field. The will, in short, is not opposed to desire, though rational desire may be opposed to sensuous desire. "By various artifices, then," Leibniz concludes, "we become masters of ourselves, and can make ourselves think and do that which we ought to will, and which reason ordains." Such is the summary of Leibniz's analysis of the elements and mechanism of volition. There was not much psychology existing at the time which could aid him in such an acute and subtle account; only in Aristotle could he have found much help. On the other hand, it has been so generally incorporated into current psychology that we may seem to have wasted space in repeating truisms.

Of moral action, however, we have as yet heard nothing. We have an account of a psychological mechanism; but for what ethical end does this work, and by what method? This question may best be answered by turning in more detail to the question of the "freedom of the will." Freedom in the sense of arbitrary choice Leibniz wholly rejects, as we have seen. It is inconsistent with at least two of his fundamental principles; those, namely, of sufficient reason, and of continuity. "Everything that occurs must have a sufficient reason for its occurrence." This oft-repeated dictum of Leibniz, the logical way of stating the complete rationality of experience, would be shattered into fragments by collision with groundless choice. It conflicts equally (indeed for the same reason) with the principle of continuity. "The present is pregnant with the future." "Nature never makes leaps." "An absolute equilibrium is a chimera." "The soul is never wholly at rest." These are only various ways of saying that the notion of arbitrary or unmotivated choice rests upon the assumption that there is a complete break in the life of the soul, so that it is possible for something to happen which bears no organic relation to anything that precedes. The notion of a state of the soul without motives, followed by the irruption of a certain line of conduct, the notion of an equilibrium broken by arbitrary choice, is simply the counterpart of the idea of a vacuum. All that makes Leibniz reject the latter conception makes it impossible for him to accept the former.

This should not be interpreted to mean that Leibniz denied the "freedom of the will." What he denied is a notion of freedom which seemed to him at once unverifiable, useless, and irrational. There is a conception of freedom which Leibniz not only accepts, but insists upon. Such a notion of freedom is indeed his ethical ideal. Its three traits are contingency, spontaneity, and rationality of action. How action can be at the same time contingent and determined is perhaps difficult to understand; but Leibniz takes the position that it is. His first step is to distinguish between physical, mathematical, metaphysical, and moral necessity. There are truths which are eternal, truths which are absolutely necessary, because their opposites involve contradiction. They cannot be violated without involving us in absurdity. There are other truths which are "positive," that is, ordained for good reason. These truths may be *a priori*, or rational, and not merely empirical; for they have been chosen for reasons of advantage. God always chooses and ordains the best of a number of possibilities; but he does it, not because the opposite is impossible, but because it is inferior. Truths whose opposites are impossible have metaphysical and mathematical necessity. Positive truths have moral necessity. The principle of causation *must* be true; the three interior angles of a triangle *must* be equal to two right angles. But that God shall choose the better of two courses is a moral necessity only. It involves no absolute logical contradiction to conceive him choosing some other way. Upon moral necessity depends the physical. The particular laws of nature are necessary, not because their opposites are logically absurd, but because these laws are most in accordance with the general principles of good and order, in agreement with which God chooses. Physical and moral action is therefore in all cases contingent. (Contingency does not of itself, of course, constitute freedom, but conjoined with the characteristics of rationality and spontaneity, does so.)

Necessity, in short, is based upon the principle of logical contradiction; contingency upon that of sufficient reason. Since our actions are in no case necessitated in such a way that their opposite is self-contradictory, or, put positively, since our actions are always determined by the choice of that which seems best, our actions are contingent. Occasionally Leibniz puts the matter in a much simpler way, and one which brings out the essential element more clearly than the foregoing distinction. Some facts are determined by the principle of physical causation; others by that of final causation. Some, in other words, are necessary as the mechanical outcome of their antecedents; others are necessary as involved in the reaching of a given end. It is simply the Aristotelian distinction between efficient and teleological causation. Human action is determined, since it always has a motive or reason; it is contingent, because it springs from this reason and not from its temporal antecedents. It is, in short, determined, but it is also free.

It does not require much analysis, however, to see that this distinction, in whatever way it be put, really has no significance, except as it points to the other marks of freedom, — spontaneity and rationality. As we shall see, Leibniz makes and can make no absolute distinction between truths of reason and truths of fact. The contingent and the necessary are one at bottom. To us with our limited intelligence it does indeed often appear as if no contradiction were involved in the former, — as if, for example, a man could turn either to right or left without there being any logical contradiction in either case; but this is because of our defective insight. An intelligence cognizant of the whole matter could see that one action would contradict some truth involved in the constitution of the universe. The source of the contingent and changing is in the necessary and eternal. Thus it is that although Leibniz at one time says that "neither one's self nor any other spirit more enlightened could demonstrate that the opposite of a given action (like going out in preference to staying in) involves contradiction," at another time he says that "a perfect knowledge of all the circumstances, internal and external, would enable any one to foresee" the decision in a given case. If that be so, any other action must be impossible; that is, according to Leibniz's invariable logic, imply contradiction.

We get the same result if we consider the relation of final and efficient causes. It is only when speaking in a very general way that Leibniz opposes action as determined by precedent activities to that directed towards the attainment of an end. He does not really mean that *some* action is physical, while *other* is teleological. He cannot suppose that some action has an antecedent cause, while other has a purpose. The very essence of his thought is that action is both mechanical and teleological; that all action follows in a law of order from precedent action, and that all fulfils a certain spiritual function. The distinction is not, with Leibniz, one between two kinds of action, but between two ways of looking at every action. The desire to go rather than to stay, has its efficient cause; the movements by which the desire is executed, have their final cause. The truth of the matter seems to be that Leibniz in his desire to guard against being thought a fatalist, or one denying all freedom, uses terms which are compatible only with a freedom of indifference. So in his statement that man's action is free because "contingent," he seems actuated rather by a wish to avoid the hateful term "necessity" than by considerations strictly in harmony with his own principles.

Had he confined his use of the term "contingent," however, simply to re-stating the fact that human action is spontaneous, no such apparent contradiction would have presented itself. Human actions may be called contingent, as physical actions are not, because the latter always seem to be externally determined, while the former are internally directed. Motions act from without; motives from within. The cause of the falling of a stone lies outside it; the source of a desire which moves to action is from the mind itself. We are thus introduced to contingency as a synonym of "spontaneity."

Kuno Fischer calls attention to the fact that Spinoza and Leibniz both use the same sort of illustration to show the non-arbitrary character of human action, but the same illustration with a difference; and in the difference he finds the distinction between the two philosophies. Spinoza says that a stone falling to the ground, if endowed with consciousness, might imagine itself following its own will in falling. Leibniz says that a magnetic needle similarly endowed might imagine that it turned towards the north simply because it wished. Both examples are used to illustrate the folly of relying upon the immediate "testimony" of consciousness. But the example of Spinoza is that of an object, all whose movements are absolutely necessitated from without; the example of Leibniz is that of an object whose activity, though following law, and not caprice, is apparently initiated from within. Of course in reality the movements of the magnetic needle are just as much externally conditioned as those of the stone; but the appearance of self-action in the latter case may serve at least to exemplify what is meant by spontaneity as attributed to human action.

It must be noticed at the outset that spontaneity belongs to every simple substance. We have only to recall the doctrine of monads. These suffer nothing from without, all their activity is the expression, is the unfolding, of their own law. "By nature," Leibniz says, "every simple substance has perceptions, and its individuality consists in the permanent law which forms the succession of its perceptions, that are born naturally one of another. Hence it is not necessary for it to receive any physical influence from without; and therefore the soul has in itself a perfect spontaneity in such a way that its actions depend only upon God and itself." Or if we put the matter in its connection with his psychology rather than with his metaphysics, it is true that our actions are determined by our motives; but motives are not forces without the soul, they are forces *of* the soul. In acting according to motives the soul is simply acting according to its own laws. A desire is not an impulsion from an external cause; it is the expression of an inward tendency. To say that the soul acts from the strongest desire is simply to say, from this standpoint, that it manifests the most real part of itself, not that it obeys a foreign force. Impulses, desires, motives, are all psychical; they admit of no description or explanation except in their relation to the soul itself. Thus when Leibniz compares, as he often does, motives to weights acting upon a balance, we are to remember that the balance is not to be conceived as the soul, and the weights as energies outside it, but that this is only a way of picturing what is going on *within* the soul itself. The soul may be a mechanism, but it is a self-directing and self-executing mechanism. To say that human action is free because it is spontaneous, is to say that it follows an immanent principle, that it is independent of foreign influences,—in a word, that it is self-determined.

But here again it seems as if Leibniz had stated a principle altogether too wide to throw any light upon the nature of moral freedom. Spontaneity is no more an attribute of human activity than it is of all real activity. Every monad, even the unconscious, as truly follows its own law without interference from without as does man himself. If the spontaneity of action constitutes its morality, we are not in a condition to ascribe morality to man any more than to any real thing. We are thus thrown back again upon the conception of rationality as the final and decisive trait of freedom and of ethical conduct. Just as "contingency" gets a moral import only in connection with conscious ends of action, so "spontaneity" comes within the moral realm only when conjoined to reason.

Why is there this close connection between reason and freedom? The reader has only to recall what was said of Leibniz's theory of causality to get a glimpse into their unity. Causality is not a matter of physical influence, but of affording the reason in virtue of which some fact is what it is. This applies of course to the relation of the soul and the body. "So far as the soul is perfect and has distinct ideas, God has accommodated the body to it; so far as the soul is imperfect and its ideas are confused, God has accommodated the soul to the body. In the former case the body always responds to the demands of the soul; in the latter the soul is moved by the passions which are born of the sensuous ideas. Each is thought to act upon the other in the measure of its perfection [that is, degree of activity], since God has adjusted one thing to another according to its perfection or imperfection. Activity and passivity are always reciprocal in created things, because a portion of the reasons which serve to explain what goes on is in one substance, and another portion in the other. This is what makes us call one active, the other passive."

If we translate these ideas out of their somewhat scholastic phraseology, the meaning is that the self-activity of any substance is accurately measured by the extent to which it contains the reasons for its own actions; and conversely, that it is dependent or enslaved just so far as it has its reasons beyond itself. Sensations, sensuous impulses, represent, as we have seen before, the universe only in a confused and inarticulate way. They are knowledge which cannot give an account of itself. They represent, in short, that side of mind which may be regarded as affected, or the limitation of mind,— its want of activity. So far as the mind acts from these sensations and the feelings which accompany them, it is ideally determined from without; it is a captive to its own states; it is in a condition of passivity. In all action, therefore, which occurs from a sensuous basis, the soul is rightly regarded as unfree.

On the other hand, just in the degree in which distinctness is introduced into the sensations, so that they are not simply experienced as they come, but are related to one another so that their reason for existence, their spiritual meaning, is ascertained, just in that degree is the soul master of itself. In Leibniz's own words: "Distinct knowledge or intelligence has its place in the true use of reason, while the senses furnish confused ideas. Hence we can say that we are free from slavery just in the degree that we act with distinct knowledge, but are subject to our passions in just the degree that our ideas are confused;" that is, not really representative of things as they are. "Intelligence is the soul of liberty."

This psychological explanation rests, of course, upon the foundation principle of the Leibnizian philosophy. Spirit is the sole reality, and spirit is activity. But there are various degrees of activity, and each grade lower than the *purus actus* may be rightfully regarded as in so far passive. This relative passivity or unreality constitutes the material and hence the sensuous world. One who has not insight into truth, lives and acts in this world of comparative unreality; he is in bondage to it. From this condition of slavery only reason, the understanding of things as they are, can lift one. The rational man is free because he acts, in the noble words of Spinoza, *sub specie æternitatis*. He acts in view of the eternal truth of things, — as God himself would act.

God alone, it further follows, is wholly free. In him alone are understanding and will wholly one.

In him the true and the good are one; while every created intelligence is subject in some degree to sensuous affection, to passion. "In us, besides the judgment of the understanding, there is always mixed some unreal idea of the sensation which gives birth to passions and impulses, and these traverse the judgment of the practical understanding." Freedom, in fine, is not a ready made garment with which all men are clothed to do with as they will. It is the ethical ideal; it is something to be attained; it is action in conformity with reason, or insight into the spiritual nature of reality and into its laws; it is not the starting-point, it is the goal. Only with a great price do men purchase such freedom. It will be noticed at once that Leibniz comes very close to Plato in his fundamental ethical ideas. The unity of virtue and reason, of virtue and freedom, — these are thoroughly Platonic conceptions. To both Plato and Leibniz reason is the ethical ideal because it is the expression of, nay, rather, *is* the reality of the universe; while all else is, as Leibniz says, imperfect or unreal, since it is not an activity, or, as Plato says, a mixture of Being and Non-Being. Again, to both man bears a similar relation to this spiritual reality. In Plato's words, he participates in the Ideas; in those of Leibniz he reflects, as a mirror, the universe. To both, in a word, the reality, the true-self of the individual, is the spiritual universe of which it is an organic member. To both, therefore, man obtains freedom or self-realization only as he realizes his larger and more comprehensive identity with the Reason of the universe. With both, knowledge is the good, ignorance is the evil. No man is voluntarily bad, but only through lack of knowledge of the true Good. Leibniz, however, with a more developed psychology, supplements Plato in the point where the latter had the most difficulty, — the possibility of the feelings or of a love of pleasure overcoming knowledge of the good. This possibility Plato was compelled to deny, while Leibniz, by his subtle identifying of the passions with lack of knowledge, or with confused knowledge, can admit it. "It is an imperfection of our freedom," says Leibniz, "which causes us to choose evil rather than good, — a greater evil rather than the less, the less good rather than the greater. This comes from the *appearances* of good and evil which deceive us; but God, who is perfect knowledge, is always led to the true and to the best good, that is, to the true and absolute good."

It only remains briefly to apply these conceptions to some specific questions of moral actions. Locke asks whether there are practical innate ideas, and denies them, as he denies theoretical. Leibniz, in replying, recognizes two kinds of "innate" practical principles, one of which is to be referred to the class of instincts, the other to that of maxims. Primarily, and probably wholly in almost all men, moral truths take the rank of instincts alone. All men aim at the Good; it is impossible to think of man wilfully seeking his own evil. The methods, the means of reaching this Good, are implanted in men as instincts. These instincts, when brought to the light of reason and examined, become *maxims* of action; they lose their particular and impulsive character, and become universal and deliberate principles. Thus Leibniz is enabled to answer the various objections which are always brought against any "intuitive" theory of moral actions, — the variability of men's moral beliefs and conduct in different countries and at different times. Common instincts, but at first instincts only, are present in all men whenever and wherever they live. These instincts may readily be "resisted by men's passions, obscured by prejudice, and changed by custom." The moral instincts are always the basis of moral action, but "custom, tradition, education" become mixed with them. Even when so confounded, however, the instinct will generally prevail, and custom is, upon the whole, on the side of right rather than wrong, so that Leibniz thinks there is a sense in which all men have one common morality.

But these moral instincts, even when pure, are not ethical science. This is innate, Leibniz says, only in the sense in which arithmetic is innate, — it depends upon demonstrations which reason furnishes. Leibniz does not, then, oppose intuitive and demonstrative, as sometimes happens. Morality is *practically* intuitive in the sense that all men tend to aim at the Good, and have an instinctive feeling of what makes towards the Good. It is *theoretically* demonstrative, since it does not become a science until Reason has an insight into the nature of the Good, and ascertains the fixed laws which are tributary to it. Moral principles are *not* intuitive in the sense that they are immediately discovered as separate principles by some one power of the soul called "conscience." Moral laws are intuitive, he says, "as the *consequences* of our own development and our true well-being." Here we may well leave the matter. What is to be said in detail of Leibniz's ethics will find its congenial home in what we have to say of his theology.

CHAPTER VII.

MATTER AND ITS RELATION TO SPIRIT.

LOCKE'S account of innate ideas and of sensation is only preparatory to a discussion of the ideas got by sensation. His explanation of the mode of knowledge leads up to an explanation of the things known. He remains true to his fundamental idea that before we come to conclusions about any matters we must "examine our own ability." He deals first with ideas got by the senses, whether by some one or by their conjoint action. Of these the ideas of solidity, of extension, and of duration are of most concern to us. They form as near an approach to a general philosophy of nature as may be found anywhere in Locke. They are, too, the germ from which grew the ideas of matter, of space, and of time, which, however more comprehensive in scope and more amply worked out in detail, characterize succeeding British thought, and which are reproduced to-day by Mr. Spencer.

"The idea of solidity we receive by our touch." "The ideas we get by more than one sense are of space or extension, figure, rest, and motion." These sentences contain the brief statement of the chief contention of the sensational school. Locke certainly was not conscious when he wrote them that they were the expression of ideas which should resolve the world of matter and of space into a dissolving series of accidentally associated sensations; but such was none the less the case. When he writes, "If any one asks me what solidity is, I send him to his senses to inform him," he is preparing the way for Berkeley, and for a denial of all reality beyond the feelings of the individual mind. When he says that "we get the idea of space both by sight and touch," this statement, although appearing truistic, is none the less the source of the contention of Hume that even geometry contains no necessary or universal elements, but is an account of sensible appearances, relative, as are all matters of sensation.

Locke's ideas may be synopsized as follows: It is a sufficient account of solidity to say that it is got by touch and that it arises from the resistance found in bodies to the entrance of any other body. "It is that which hinders the approach of two bodies when they are moved towards one another." If not identical with matter, it is at all events its most essential property. "This of all others seems the idea most intimately connected with and essential to body, so as nowhere else to be found or imagined, but only in matter." It is, moreover, the source of the other properties of matter. "Upon the solidity of bodies depend their mutual impulse, resistance, and protrusion." Solidity, again, "is so inseparable an idea from body that upon that depends its filling of space, its contact, impulse, and communication of motion upon impulse." It is to be distinguished, therefore, from hardness, for hardness is relative and derived, various bodies having various degrees of it; while solidity consists in utter exclusion of other bodies from the space possessed by any one, so that the hardest body has no more solidity than the softest.

The close connection between solidity and matter makes it not only possible, but necessary, to distinguish between matter and extension as against the Cartesians, who had identified them. In particular Locke notes three differences between these notions. Extension includes neither solidity nor resistance; its parts are inseparable from one another both really and mentally, and are immovable; while matter has solidity, its parts are mutually separable, and may be moved *in* space. From this distinction between space and matter it follows, according to Locke, that there is such a thing as a vacuum, or that space is not necessarily a plenum of matter. Matter is that which fills space; but it is entirely indifferent to space whether or not it is filled. Space is occupied by matter, but there is no essential relation between them. Solidity is the essence of matter; emptiness is the characteristic of space. "The idea of space is as distinct from that of solidity as it is from that of scarlet color. It is true, solidity cannot exist without extension, neither can scarlet color exist without extension; but this hinders not that they are *distinct ideas*."

Thus there is fixed for us the idea of space as

well as of matter. It is a distinct idea; that is, absolute or independent in itself, having no intrinsic connection with phenomena *in* space. Yet it is got through the senses. How that can be a matter of sensation which is not only not material, but has no connection in itself with matter, Locke does not explain. He thinks it sufficient to say that we see distance between bodies of different color just as plainly as we see the colors. Space is, therefore, a purely immediate idea, containing no more organic relation to intelligence than it has to objects. We get the notion of time as we do that of space, excepting that it is the observation of internal states and not of external objects which furnishes the material of the idea. Time has two elements, — succession and duration. "Observing what passes in the mind, how of our ideas there in train some constantly vanish, and others begin to appear, we come by the idea of succession, and by observing a distance in the parts of this succession we get the idea of duration." Whether, however, time is something essentially empty, having no relation to the events which fill it, as space is essentially empty, without necessary connection with the objects which fill it, is a question Locke does not consider. In fact, the gist of his ideas upon this point is as follows: there is actually an objective space or pure emptiness; employing our senses, we get the idea of this space. There is actually an objective time; employing reflection, we perceive it. There is not the slightest attempt to form a philosophy of them, or to show their function in the construction of an intelligible world, except in the one point of the absolute independence of matter and space.

It cannot be said that Leibniz criticises the minor points of Locke in such a way as to throw much light upon them, or that he very fully expresses his own ideas about them. He contents himself with declaring that while the senses may give instances of space, time, and matter, and may suggest to intelligence the stimuli upon which intelligence realizes these notions from itself, they cannot be the source of these notions themselves; finding the evidence of this in the sciences of geometry, arithmetic, and pure physics. For these sciences deal with the notions of space, time, and matter, giving necessary and demonstrative ideas concerning them, which the senses can never legitimate. He further denies the supposed absoluteness or independence of space, matter, and motion. Admitting, indeed, the distinction between extension and matter, he denies that this distinction suffices to prove the existence, or even the possibility, of a vacuum, and ends with a general reference to his doctrine of pre-established harmony, as serving to explain these matters more fully and more accurately.

Leibniz has, however, a complete philosophy of nature. In his other writing, he explains the ideas of matter and force in their dependence upon his metaphysic, or doctrine of spiritual entelechies. The task does not at first sight appear an easy one. The reality, according to Leibniz, is purely spiritual, does not exist in space nor time, and is a principle of activity following its own law, — that of reflecting the universe of spiritual relations. How from this world of ideal, unextended, and non-temporal dynamic realities we are to pass over to a material world of extension, with its static existence in space, and transitory passage in time, is a question challenging the whole Leibnizian system. It is a question, however, for which Leibniz himself has provided an answer. We may not regard it as adequate; we may think that he has not truly derived the material world from his spiritual principles: but at all events he asked himself the question, and gave an answer. We shall investigate this answer by arranging what Leibniz has said under the heads of: matter as a metaphysical principle; matter as a physical phenomenon; and the relation of phenomena to absolute reality, or of the physical to the metaphysical. In connection with the second head, particularly, we shall find it necessary to discuss what Leibniz has said about space, time, and motion.

Wolff, who put the ideas of Leibniz into systematic shape, did it at the expense of almost all their significance. He took away the air of paradox, of remoteness, that characterized Leibniz's thought, and gave it a popular form. But its depth and suggestiveness vanished in the process. Unfortunately, Wolff's presentations of the philosophy of Leibniz have been followed by others, to whom it seemed a dull task to follow out the intricacies of a thought nowhere systematically expressed. This has been especially the case as concerns the Leibnizian doctrine of matter. A superficial interpretation of certain passages in Leibniz has led to an almost universal misunderstanding about it. Leibniz frequently says that since matter is composite or complex, it follows that there must be something simple as its basis, and this simple something is the monad. The misinterpretation just spoken of consists in supposing that Leibniz meant that matter as composite is made up of monads as simple; that the monad and matter are facts of the same order, the latter being only an aggregate, or continued collection of the former. It interpreted the conception of Leibniz in strict analogy with the atomic theory of Lucretius, excepting that it granted that the former taught that the ultimate atom, the component of all complex forms of matter, has position only, not extension, its essence consisting in its exercise of force, not in its mere space occupancy. The monad was thus considered to be *in* space, or at least conditioned by space relations, as is a mathematical point, although not itself spatial in the sense of being extended. Monad and matter were thus represented as facts of the same kind or genus, having their difference only in their relative isolation or aggregation.

But Leibniz repudiated this idea, and that not only by the spirit of his teaching, but in express words. Monads "are not ingredients or constituents of matter," he says, "but only *conditions* of it."

"Monads can no more be said to be parts of bodies, or to come in contact with them, or to compose them, than can souls or mathematical points." "Monads *per se* have *no* situation relative to one another." An increase in the number of created monads, he says again, if such a thing could be supposed, would no more increase the amount of matter in existence, than mathematical points added to a line would increase its length. And again: "There is no nearness or remoteness among monads; to say that they are gathered in a point or are scattered in space, is to employ mental fictions, *in trying to imagine what can only be thought.*" The italicized words give the clew to the whole discussion. To make monads of the same order as corporeal phenomena, is to make them sensible, or capable of being imaged, or conditioned by space and time, — three phrases which are strictly correlative. But the monads can only be thought, — that is, their qualities are ideal, not sensible; they can be realized only by reason, not projected in forms having spatial outline and temporal habitation, that is, in images. Monads and material things, in other words, are facts of two distinct orders; they are related as the rational or spiritual and the physical or sensible. Matter is no more composed of monads than it is of thoughts or of logical principles. As Leibniz says over and over again: Matter, space, time, motion are only phenomena, although phenomena *bene fundata*, — phenomena, that is, having their rational basis and condition. The monads, on the other hand, are not appearances, they are realities.

Having freed our minds from the supposition that it is in any way possible to form an image or picture of the monad; having realized that it is wholly false to suppose that monads occupy position in space, and then by their continuity fill it, and make extended matter, — we must attempt to frame a correct theory of the nature of matter and its relation to the monad. We shall do this only as we realize that "matter," so far as it has any reality, or so far as it has any real *fundamentum*, must be something ideal, or, in Leibniz's language, "metaphysical." As he says over and over again, the only realities are the substances or spiritual units of activity, to which the name "monad" is given. In the inquiry, then, after such reality as matter may have, we must betake ourselves to this unit of living energy.

Although every monad is active, it is not entirely active. There is, as we have already seen, an infinite scale of substances; and since substance is equivalent to activity, this is saying that there is an infinite scale of activities. God alone is *purus actus*, absolute energy, untouched by passivity or receptivity. Every other being has the element of incompleteness, of inadequacy; it does not completely represent the universe. In this passivity consists its finitude, so that Leibniz says that not even God himself could deprive monads of it, for this would be to make them equal to himself. In this passivity, incompleteness, or finitude, consists what we call matter. Leibniz says that he can understand what Plato meant when he called matter something essentially imperfect and transitory. Every finite monad is a union of two principles,—those of activity and of passivity. "I do not admit," says Leibniz, "that there are souls existing simply by themselves, or that there are created spirits detached from all body. God alone is above all matter, since he is its author; creatures freed from matter would be at the same time detached from the universal connection of things, and, as it were, deserters from the general order." And again, "Beings have a nature which is both active and passive; *that is*, material and immaterial." And again, he says that every created monad requires both an entelechy, or principle of activity, and matter. "Matter is essential to any entelechy, and can never be separated from it, since matter *completes* it." In short, the term "monad" is equivalent to the term "entelechy" only when applied to God. In every other monad, the entelechy, or energy, is but one factor. "Matter, or primitive passive power, completes the entelechy, or primitive active power, so that it becomes a perfect substance, or monad." On the other hand, of course, matter, as the passive principle, is a mere potentiality or abstraction, considered in itself. It is real only in its union with the active principle. Matter, he says, "cannot exist without immaterial substances." "To every particular portion of matter belongs a particular *form;* that is, a soul, a spirit." To this element of matter, considered as an abstraction, in its distinction from soul, Leibniz, following the scholastics, and ultimately Aristotle, gives the name, "first" or "bare" matter. The same influence is seen in the fact that he opposes this element of matter to "form," or the active principle.

Our starting-point, therefore, for the consideration of matter is the statement that it is receptivity, the capacity for being affected, which always constitutes matter. But what is meant by "receptivity"? To answer this question we must return to what was said about the two activities of the monad, — representation, or perception, and appetition, — and to the difference between confused and distinct ideas. The monad has appetition so far as it determines itself from within to change, so far as it follows an internal principle of energy. It is representative so far as it is determined from without, so far as it receives impressions from the universe. Yet we have learned to know that in one sense everything occurs from the spontaneity of the monad itself; it receives no influence or influxus from without; everything comes from its own depths, or is appetition. But, on the other hand, all that which so comes forth is only a mirroring or copying of the universe. The whole content of the appetition is representation. Although the monad works spontaneously, it is none the less determined in its activities to produce only reflections or images of the world. In this way appetition and representation appear to be identical. The monad is determined from within, indeed, but it is determined to exactly the same results as if wholly determined from without. What light, then, can be thrown from this distinction upon the nature of matter?

None, unless we follow Leibniz somewhat farther. If we do, we shall see that the soul is regarded as appetitive, or self-active, so far as it has clear and distinct ideas. If the monad reaches distinct consciousness, it has knowledge of self, — that is, of the nature of pure spirit, — or, what again is equivalent to this, of the nature of reality as it universally is. Such knowledge is knowledge of God, of substance, of unity, of pure activity, and of all the innate ideas which elevate the confused perceptions of sense into science. Distinct consciousness is therefore equivalent to self-activity, and this to recognition of God and the universal. But if knowledge is confused, it is not possible to see it in its relations to self; it cannot be analyzed; the rational or ideal element in it is concealed from view. In confused ideas, therefore, the soul appears to be passive; being passive, to be determined from without. This determination from without is equivalent to that which is opposed to spirit or reason, and hence appears as matter. Such is in outline the Leibnizian philosophy.

It thus is clear that merely stating that matter is passivity in the monad is not the ultimate way of stating its nature. For passivity means in reality nothing but confused representations, — representations, that is, whose significance is not perceived. The true significance of every representation is found in its relation to the ego, or pure self-activity, which, through its dependent relation upon God, the absolute self-activity and ego, produces the representation from its own ideal being. So far as the soul does not have distinct recognition of relation of all representations to self, it feels them as coming from without; as foreign to spirit; in short, as matter. Leibniz thus employs exactly the same language about confused ideas that he does about passivity, or matter. It is not possible that the monad should have distinct consciousness of itself as a mirror of the whole universe, he says, "for in that case every entelechy would be God." Again, "the soul would be God if it could enter at once and with distinctness into everything occurring within it." But it is necessary "that we should have passions which consist in confused ideas, in which there is something involuntary and unknown, and which represent the body and constitute our imperfection." Again, he speaks of matter as "the *mixture* (*mélange*) of the effects of the infinite environing us." In that expression is summed up his whole theory of matter. It is a mixture; it is, that is to say, confused, aggregated, irresolvable into simple ideas. But it is a mixture of "effects of the infinite about us;" that is, it takes its rise in the true, the real, the spiritual. It only fails to represent this as it actually is. Matter, in short, is a phenomenon dependent upon inability to realize the entire spiritual character of reality. It is spirit apprehended in a confused, hesitating, and passive manner.

It is none the less a necessary phenomenon, for it is involved in the idea of a continuous gradation of monads, in the distinction between the infinite and the finite, or, as Leibniz often prefers to put it, between the "creator" and the "created." There is involved everywhere in the idea of Leibniz the conception of subordination; of a hierarchy of forms, each of which receives the law of its action from the next higher, and gives the law to the next lower. We have previously considered the element of passivity or receptivity as relating only to the monad which manifests it. It is evident, however, that what is passive in one, implies something active in another. What one receives, is what another gives. The reciprocal influence of monads upon one another, therefore, as harmonious members of one system, requires matter. More strictly speaking, this reciprocal influence *is* matter. To take away all receptivity, all passivity, from monads would be to isolate them from all relations with others; it would be to deprive them of all power of affecting or being affected by others. That is what Leibniz meant by the expression already quoted, that if monads had not matter as an element in them, "they would be, as it were, deserters from the general order." The note of unity, of organic connection, which we found to be the essence of the Leibnizian philosophy, absolutely requires, therefore, matter, or passivity.

It must be remembered that this reciprocal influence is ideal. As Leibniz remarks, "When it is said that one monad is affected by another, this is to be understood concerning its *representation* of the other. For the Author of things has so accommodated them to one another that one is said to suffer (or receive from the other) when its relative value gives way to that of the other." Or again, "the modifications of one monad are the ideal causes of the modifications of another monad, so far as there appear in one the reasons on account of which God brought about in the beginning certain modifications in another." And most definitely of all: "A creature is called active so far as it has perfection; passive in so far as it is imperfect. One creature is more perfect than another so far as there is found in it that which serves to *render the reason, a priori*, for that occurring in the other; and it is in this way that it acts upon the other."

We are thus introduced, from a new point of view and in a more concrete way, to the conception of pre-established harmony. The activity of one, the energy which gives the law to the other and makes it subordinate in the hierarchy of monads, is conceived necessarily as spirit, as soul; that which receives, which is rendered subordinate by the activity of the other, is body. The pre-established harmony is the fact that they are so related that one can receive the law of its activity from the other. Leibniz is without doubt partially responsible for the ordinary misconception of his views upon this point by reason of the illustration which he was accustomed to use; namely, of two clocks so constructed that without any subsequent regulation each always kept perfect time with the other, — as much so as if there were some actual physical connection between them. This seems to put soul and body, spirit and matter, as two co-ordinate substances, on the same level, with such natural opposition between them that some external harmony must arrange some unity of action. In causing this common idea of his theory of pre-established harmony, Leibniz has paid the penalty for attempting to do what he often reproves in others, — imagining or presenting in sensible form what can only be thought. But his other explanations show clearly enough that the pre-established harmony expresses, not a relation between two parallel substances, but a condition of dependence of lower forms of activity upon the higher for the law of their existence and activity, — in modern terms, it expresses the fact that phenomena are conditioned upon noumena; that material facts get their significance and share of reality through their relation to spirit.

We may sum up what has been said about matter as an element in the monad, or as a metaphysical principle, as follows: The existence of matter is not only not opposed to the fundamental ideas of Leibniz, but is a necessary deduction from them. It is a necessity of the principle of continuity; for this requires an infinity of monads, alike indeed in the universal law of their being, but unlike, each to each, in the specific coloring or manifestation of this law. The principle of organic unity requires that there be as many real beings as possible participating in and contributing to it. It is necessary, again, in order that there may be reciprocal influence or connection among the monads. Were it not for the material element in the monad, each would be a God; if each were thus infinite and absolute, there would be so many principles wholly independent and isolated. The principle of harmony would be violated. So much for the necessity of the material factor. As to its nature, it is a principle of passivity; that is, of ideal receptivity, of conformity to a law apparently not self-imposed, but externally laid down. This makes matter equivalent to a phenomenon; that is to say, to the having of confused, imperfect, inadequate ideas. To say that matter is correlative to confused ideas is to say that there is no recognition of its relation to self or to spirit. As Leibniz sometimes puts it, since there is an infinity of beings in the universe, each one of which exercises an ideal influence upon every other one of the series, it is impossible that this other one should realize their full meaning; they appear only as confused ideas, or as matter. To use language which Leibniz indeed does not employ, but which seems to convey his thought, the spirit, not seeing them as they really are, does not *find* itself in them. But matter is thus not only the confused manifestation or phenomenon of spirit, it is also its potentiality. Passivity is always relative. It does not mean complete lack of activity; that, as Leibniz says, is nothingness, and matter is not a form of nothingness. Leibniz even speaks of it as passive *power*. That is to say, there is an undeveloped or incomplete activity in what appears as matter, and this may be, — if we admit an infinity of time, — must be developed. When developed it manifests itself as it really is, as spirit. Confused ideas, as Leibniz takes pains to state, are not a genus of ideas antithetical to distinct; they differ only in degree or grade. They are on their way to become distinct, or else they are distinct ideas which have fallen back into an "involved" state of being. Matter, therefore, is not absolutely opposed to spirit, — on the one hand because it is the manifestation, the phenomenon, of spirit; on the other, because it is the potentiality of spirit, capable of sometime realizing the whole activity implied in it, but now latent.

Thus it is that Leibniz says that everything is "full" of souls or monads. What appears to be lifeless is in reality like a pond full of fishes, like a drop of water full of infusoria. Everything is organic down to the last element. More truly, there is no last element. There is a true infinity of organic beings wrapped up in the slightest speck of apparently lifeless matter. These illustrations, like many others which Leibniz uses, are apt to suggest that erroneous conception of the relation of monads to spirit which we were obliged, in Leibniz's name, to correct at the outset, — the idea, namely, that matter is composed, in a spatial or mechanical way, of monads. But after the foregoing explanations we can see that what Leibniz means when he says that every portion of matter is full of entelechies or souls, like a garden full of plants, is that there is an absolute continuity of spiritual principles, each having its ideal relation with every other. There is no point of matter which does not represent in a confused way the entire universe. It is therefore as infinite in its activities as the universe. In idea also it is capable of representing in distinct consciousness, or as a development of its own self-activity, each of these infinite activities.

In a word, every created or finite being may be regarded as matter or as spirit, according as it is accounted for by its external relations, as the reasons for what happen in it are to be found elsewhere than in its own explicit activity, or according as it shows clearly in itself the reasons for its own modifications, and also accounts for changes occurring in other beings. The externally conditioned is matter; the internally conditioned, the self-explanatory, is self-active, or spirit. Since all external relations are finally dependent on organic; since the ultimate source of all explanation must be that which is its own reason; since the ultimate source of all activity must be that which is self-active, — the final reason or source of matter is spirit.

CHAPTER VIII.

MATERIAL PHENOMENA AND THEIR REALITY.

WE have seen the necessity and nature of matter as deductions from the fundamental principles of Leibniz. We have seen that matter is a phenomenon or manifestation of spirit in an imperfect and confused way. But why should it appear as moving, as extended, as resisting, as having cohesion, with all the concrete qualities which always mark it? Is there any connection between these particular properties of matter as physical, and its "metaphysical" or ideal character? These are the questions which now occupy us. Stated more definitely, they take the following form: Is there any essential connection between the properties of matter as a metaphysical element, and its properties as a sensible fact of experience? Leibniz holds that there is. He does not, indeed, explicitly take the ground that we can deduce *a priori* all the characteristics of matter as a fact of actual experience from its rational notion, but he thinks we can find a certain analogy between the two, that the sensible qualities are images or reflexes of the spiritual qualities, witnessing, so far as possible, to their origin in pure energy.

His position is as follows: that which in the monad is activity or substantial, is, in sensible matter, motion. That which in the monad is lack of a given activity, that which constitutes its subordinate position in the hierarchy of monads, is, in the sphere of material things, inertia. That which in the spiritual world is the individuality of monads, making each forever ideally distinct from every other, is, in the phenomenal realm, resistance or impenetrability. The perfect continuity of monads in the *mundus intelligibilis* has also its counterpart in the *mundus sensibilis* in the diffusion or extension of physical things.

Instead of following out this analogy directly, it will rather be found convenient to take up Leibniz's thought in its historical connection. We have already alluded to the fact that he began as a Cartesian, and that one of the first ideas which repelled him from that system of thought was the notion that the essence of matter is extension. His earliest philosophical writings, as he was gradually coming to the thoughts which thereafter dominated him, are upon this point. In general, his conclusions are as follows: If matter were extension, it would be incapable of passion or of action. Solidity, too, is a notion entirely opposed to the conception of mere extension. The idea of matter as extension contradicts some of the known laws of motion. It requires that the quantity of motion remain unchanged whenever two bodies come in contact, while as matter of fact it is the quantity of energy, that which the motion is capable of effecting, that remains unchanged; or, as he more often puts the objection, the Cartesian notion of matter requires that matter be wholly indifferent to motion, that there be nothing in it which resists motion when imparted. But, says Leibniz, there is something resisting, that to which Keppler gave the name "inertia." It is not found to be true if one body impacts upon another that the second moves without diminishing the velocity or changing the direction of the first. On the other hand, just in proportion to the size of the second body, it resists and changes the motion of the first, up to the point of causing the first to rebound if small in comparison. And when it was replied that the retardation was due to the fact that the force moving the first body had now to be divided between two, Leibniz answered that this was simply to give up the contention, and besides the notion of extension to use that of force. If extension were the essence of matter, it should be possible to deduce all the properties of matter, or at least to account for them all, from it. But since, as just seen, this does not enable us to account for any of them, since for any of its concrete qualities we have to fall back on force, it is evident where the true essence of matter is to be found.

Leibniz has another argument of a logical nature, as those already referred to are of a physical: "Those who claim that extension is a substance, reverse the order of words as well as of thoughts. Besides extension there must be a subject which is extended; that is to say, something to which it belongs to be repeated or continued. For extension is nothing but a repetition or continued multiplication of that which is spread out, — it is a plurality, a continuity, a co-existence of parts. Consequently, extension does not suffice to explain the nature of the repeated or manifold substance, of which the notion is anterior to that of its repetition." Extension, in other words, is nothing substantial, it is not something which can exist by itself; it is only a quality, a property, a mode of being. It is always relative to something which has extension. As Leibniz says elsewhere: "I insist that extension is only an *abstraction*, and requires something which is extended. It presupposes some quality, some attribute, some nature in a subject which is extended, diffused, or continued. Extension is a diffusion of this quality. For example, in milk there is an extension or diffusion of whiteness; in the diamond an extension or diffusion of hardness; in body in general a diffusion of antitypia or materiality. There is accordingly in body something anterior to extension."

From the physical side, therefore, we find it impossible to account for the concrete properties of material phenomena from extension; on the logical we find that the idea of extension is always relative to that which is extended. What is that which is to be considered as the bearer of extension and the source of physical qualities? We are led back to the point at which we left the matter in the last chapter. It is force, and force both passive and active. Leibniz uses the term "matter" in at least three senses: it is the metaphysical element of passive force *in* the monad; it is the monad itself considered as, upon the whole, externally conditioned or unconscious; and it is the phenomenon resulting from the aggregation of the monads in the second sense. The first is naked matter, and is a pure abstraction; the second is the monad as material, as opposed to the monad, as soul; the third is clothed, or second matter, or, concretely, body, *corpus*. The first is unreal by itself; the second is one phase of substance; the third is not substantial, but is a reality, though a phenomenal one. It is from the substantial monad that we are to explain the two things now demanding explanation,—that element in *bodies* (matter in third sense) which is the source of their physical properties, and that which is the subject, the carrier, so to speak, of extension.

That of which we are in search as the source of the physical qualities of bodies is motion. This is not force, but its "image." It is force, says Leibniz, that "is the real element in motion; that is to say, it is that element which out of the present state induces a change in the future state." As force, in other words, is the causal activity which effects the development of one "representation" of a monad out of another, so motion, in the realm of phenomena, is not only change, but change which is continuous and progressive, each new position being dependent upon the foregoing, and following out of it absolutely without break.

Motion, therefore, is the manifestation of the ideal unity of substance, — a unity not of mere static inherence, but of a continuous process of activity. It is from this standpoint that Leibniz accounts for the so-called transference of motion from one body to another upon contact. The ordinary view of this, which looks at it as if one body loses the motion which another body gains, Leibniz ridicules, saying that those who hold this view seem to think that motion is a kind of thing, resembling, perchance, salt dissolved in water. The right view, on the other hand, does away with all appearance of mystery in the carrying over of motion from one body to another, for it recognizes that continuity is the very essence of motion, and that we do not have two things and a third process, but that the two bodies are phases or elements in one and the same system of movement.

Starting from this idea of motion, then, Leibniz is to account for the actual qualities of matter as found in experience. These are the form, magnitude, cohesion, resistance, and the purely sensible qualities of objects. "First" matter, that is, abstract matter, may be conceived, according to Leibniz, as perfectly homogeneous, a "subtle fluid," in his words, without any distinction of parts or of solidity. But this *is* an abstract notion. It is what matter would be without motion. Motion necessarily differentiates this plenum of homogeneity, and thus causes distinctions of figure (that is, boundaries of parts) and varieties of cohesion, or the varying solidity and fluidity of bodies. The latter difference is indeed the ultimate one. The principle of continuity or gradation, as applied to motion, makes it necessary that motions should not be in any two places of exactly the same energy. The result is that the original fluid matter is everywhere differently divided. Motion, entering into the uniform plenum, introduces distinction; it causes so much of the matter as is affected by a given movement to collect together and form in appearance a coherent body, as opposed to surrounding bodies which are affected by different degrees of energy. But even this is only approximate; the same principle of continuity must be applied within any apparently coherent body; its parts, while, in relation to other bodies, they have the same amount of motion, are in relation to one another differently affected. There are no two having exactly the same motion; if they had, there would be no distinction between them; and thus, according to the principle of Leibniz, they would be the same.

It follows at once from this that there is in the universe no body of absolute hardness or solidity, nor of entire softness or fluidity. A perfectly solid body would be one whose system of motions could not be affected by any other system, — a body which by motion had separated itself from motion, or become absolute. This is evidently an idea which contradicts itself, for the very essence of motion is continuity or relation. A body perfectly fluid, on the other hand, would be one in which there was no resistance offered to other motions, — a body, in other words, in which there are no movements that, entering into connection with one another, form a relative opposition to other movements. It would be a body isolated or out of relation with the general system of motions, and hence an impossibility. There is no last term either of solidity or of fluidity.

It equally follows as matter of course that there is no indivisible particle of matter, — no atom. The infinity of degrees of motion implies a corresponding division of matter. As already said, it is only in contrast with other relatively constant systems of motion that any body is of uniform motion; in reality there is everywhere throughout it variety of movement, and hence complete divisibility, or rather, complete division. If Leibniz were to employ the term "atom" at all, it could be only in the sense of the modern dynamical theory (of which, indeed, he is one of the originators), according to which the atom is not defined by its spatial position and outlines, but, by the range of its effects, as the centre of energies of infinite circumference. Correlative to the non-existence of the atom is the non-existence of the vacuum. The two imply each other. The hard, limited, isolated body, having no intrinsic relations with other bodies, must have room to come into external relations with them. This empty space, which is the theatre of such accidental contacts as may happen, is the vacuum. But if bodies are originally in connection with one another, if they are in reality but differentiations of varying degrees of motion within one system of motion, then there is no necessity for the vacuum, — nay, there is no place for it. The vacuum in this case could mean only a break, a chasm, in the order of nature. According to the theory of Leibniz, "bodies" are but the dynamic divisions of the one energy that fills the universe; their separateness is not an independent possession of any one of them or of all together, but is the result of relations to the entire system. Their apparent isolation is only by reason of their actual connections. To admit a vacuum anywhere, would thus be to deny the relatedness of the parts separated by it. The theory of the atom and the vacuum are the two phases of the metaphysical assumption of an indefinite plurality of independent separate realities. The theory of Leibniz, resting as it does on the idea of a perfect unity of interrelated members, must deny both of these aspects. Were we making an extended analysis of the opposed view, it would be necessary to point out that it denies itself. For it is only *through* the vacuum that the atoms are isolated or independent, and the sole function of the vacuum is to serve as the background of the atoms. The atoms, are separated only in virtue of their connection, and the vacuum is what it is — pure emptiness — only on account of that which is in it. In short, the theory is only an abstract and incomplete way of grasping the thought of relation or mediated unity.

We have thus discovered that all motions conspire together, or form a system. But in their unity they do not cease to be motions, or variously differentiated members. Through this differentiation, or mutual reaction of motions, there comes about the appearance of boundaries, of separation. From these boundaries or terminations arise the form and size of bodies. From motion also proceeds the cohesion of bodies, in the sense that each relative system resists dissolution, or hangs together. Says Leibniz, "The motions, since they are conspiring, would be troubled by separation; and accordingly this can be accomplished only by violence and with resistance." Not only form, size, and stability depend upon motion, but also the sensible, the "secondary" qualities. "It must not be supposed that color, pain, sound, etc., are arbitrary and without relation to their causes. It is not God's way to act with so little reason and order. There is a kind of resemblance, not entire, but of relation, of order. We say, for example, 'Light is in the fire,' since there are motions in the fire which are imperceptible in their separation, but which are sensible in their conjunction or confusion; and this is what is made known in the idea of light." In other words, color, sound, etc., even pain, are still the perception of motion, but in a confused way. We thus see how thoroughly Leibniz carries back all the properties of bodies to motion.

To sum up, motion is the origin of the relative solidity, the divisibleness, the form, the size, the cohesion, or active resistance of bodies, and of their properties as made known to us in immediate sensation.

In all that has been said it has been implied that extension is already in existence; "first matter" is supposed to fill all space, and motion to determine it to take upon itself its actual concrete properties. But this "first matter," when thus spoken of, has a somewhat mythological sound, even if it be admitted that it is an abstraction. For how can an abstraction be extended in space, and how can it form, as it were, a background upon which motion displays itself? The idea of "first matter" in its relation to extension evidently demands explanation. In seeking this explanation we shall also learn about that "subject" which Leibniz said was necessarily presupposed in extension, as a concrete thing is required for a quality.

The clew to the view of Leibniz upon this point may be derived, I think, from the following quotations: —

"If it were possible to see what makes extension, that kind of extension which falls under our eyes at present would vanish, and our minds would perceive nothing else than simple realities existing in mutual externality to one another. It would be as if we could distinguish the minute particles of matter variously disposed from which a painted image is formed: if we could do it, the image, which is nothing but a phenomenon, would vanish. . . . If we think of two simple realities as both existing at the same time, but distinct from one another, we look at them as if they were outside of one another, and hence conceive them as extended."

The monads are outside of one another, not spatially, but ideally; but this reciprocal distinction from one another, if it is to appear in phenomenal mode, must take the form of an image, and the image is spatial. But if the monads were pure activity, they would *not* take phenomenal form or appear in an image. They would always be thought just as they are, — unextended activities realizing the spiritual essence of the universe. But they are not pure activity; they are passive as well. It is in virtue of this passive element that the ideal externality takes upon itself phenomenal or sensible form, and thus appears as spatial externality.

Leibniz, in a passage already quoted, refers to the diffusion of materiality or *antitypia*. This word, which is of frequent occurrence in the discussions of Leibniz, he translates generally as "impenetrability," sometimes as "passive resistance." It corresponds to the solidity or resistance of which Locke spoke as forming the essence of matter. Antitypia is the representation by a monad of the passive element in other monads. Leibniz sometimes speaks as if all created monads had in themselves antitypia, and hence extension; but he more accurately expresses it by saying that they need (*exigent*) it. This is a technical term which he elsewhere uses to express the relation of the possible to the actual. The possible "needs" the actual, not in the sense that it *necessarily* requires existence, but in the sense that when the actual gives it existence, it is the logical basis of the actual, — the actual, on the other hand, being its real complement. The passivity of the monad is therefore at once the logical basis and the possibility of the impenetrability of matter. It is owing to the passivity of the monad that it does not adequately reflect (that it is not transparent to, so to speak) the activities of other monads. In its irresponsiveness, it fails to mirror them in itself. It may be said, therefore, to be impenetrable to them. They in turn, so far as they are passive, are impenetrable to it. Now the impenetrable is, *ex vi terminis*, that which excludes, and that which excludes, not in virtue of its active elasticity, but in virtue of its mere inertia, its dead weight, as it were, of resistance. But mutual exclusion of this passive sort constitutes that which is extended. Extension is the abstract quality of this concrete subject. Such, in effect, is the deduction which Leibniz gives of body, or physical matter, from matter as metaphysical; of matter as sensible or phenomenal, from matter as ideal or as intelligible.

If we put together what has been said, it is clear that material phenomena (bodies, *corpora*, in Leibniz's phrase) simply repeat in another sphere the properties of the spiritual monad. There is a complete parallelism between every property, each to each, and this necessarily; for every property of "body" is in logical dependence upon, and a phenomenalization of, some spiritual or ideal quality. Motion is the source of all the dynamic qualities of body, and motion is the reflection of Force, that force which is Life. But this force in all finite forms is conditioned by a passive, unreceptive, unresponsive factor; and this must also have its correlate in "body." This correlate is primarily impenetrability, and secondarily extension. Thus it is that concrete body always manifests motion, indeed, but upon a background of extension, and against inertia. It never has free play; had it an unrestrained field of activity, extension would disappear, and spatial motion would vanish into ideal energy. On the other hand, were the essence of matter found in resistance or impenetrability, it would be wholly inert; it would be a monotone of extension, without variety of form or cohesion. As Leibniz puts it with reference to Locke, "body" implies motion, or impetuosity, resistance, and cohesion. Motion is the active principle, resistance the passive; while cohesion, with its various grades of completeness, which produce form, size, and solidity, is the result of their union.

Leibniz, like Plato, has an intermediary between the rational and the sensible; and as Plato found that it was mathematical relations that mediate between the permanent and unified Ideas and the changing manifold objects, so Leibniz found that the relations of space and time form the natural transition from the sphere of monads to the world of bodies. As Plato found that it was the possibility of applying mathematical considerations to the world of images that showed the participation of Ideas in them, and constituted such reality as they had, so Leibniz found that space and time formed the element of order and regularity among sense phenomena, and thus brought them into kinship with the monads and made them subjects of science. It is implied in what is here said that Leibniz distinguished between space and time on the one hand, and duration and extension on the other. This distinction, which Leibniz draws repeatedly and with great care, has been generally overlooked by his commentators. But it is evident that this leaves Leibniz in a bad plight. Mathematics, in its various forms, is the science of spatial and temporal relations. But if these are identical with the forms of duration and extension, they are purely phenomenal and sensible. The science of them, according to the Leibnizian distinction between the absolutely real and the phenomenally real, would be then a science of the confused, the imperfect, and the transitory; in fact, no science at all. But mathematics, on the contrary, is to Leibniz the type of demonstrative, conclusive science. Space and time are, in his own words, "innate ideas," and the entire science of them is the drawing out of the content of these innate — that is, rational, distinct, and eternal — ideas. But extension and duration are sensible experiences; not rational, but phenomenal;

not distinct, but confused; not eternal, but evanescent. We may be sure that this contradiction would not escape Leibniz, although it has many of his critics and historians.

It is true, however, that he occasionally uses the terms as synonymous; but this where the distinction between them has no bearing on the argument in hand, and where the context determines in what sense the term is used. The distinction which he actually makes, and to which he keeps when space and time are the subject of discussion, is that extension and duration are qualities or predicates of objects and events, while space and time are relations, or orders of existence. Extension and duration are, as he says, the *immensity*, the mass, the continuation, the repetition, of some underlying subject. But space and time are the *measure* of the mass, the rule or law of the continuation, the order or mode of the repetition. Thus immediately after the passage already quoted, in which he says that extension in body is the diffusion of materiality, just as whiteness is the diffusion of a property of milk, he goes on to say "that extension is to space as duration to time. Duration and extension are attributes of things; but space and time are to be considered, as it were, outside of things, and as serving to measure them." Still more definitely he says: "Many confound the immensity or extent of things with the space by means of which this extent is defined. Space is not the extension of body, any more than duration is its time. Things keep their extension, not always their space. Everything has its own extent and duration; but it does not have a time of its own, nor keep for its own a space." Or, as he expresses the latter idea elsewhere, space is like number, in the sense that it is indifferent to spatial things, just as number is indifferent to *res numerata*. Just as the number five is not a quality or possession of any object, or group of objects, but expresses an order or relation among them, so a given space is not the property of a thing, but expresses the order of its parts to one another. But extension, on the other hand, is a property of the given objects. While extension, therefore, must always belong to some actual thing, space, as a relation, is as applicable to possible things as to actual existences; so that Leibniz sometimes says that time and space "express possibilities." They are that which makes it possible for a definite and coherent order of experiences to exist. They determine existence in some of its relations, and as such are logically prior to any given forms of existence; while extent and duration are always qualities of some given form of existence, and hence logically derivative. Since time and space "characterize possibilities" as well as actualities, it follows as a matter of course "that they are of the nature of eternal truths, which relate equally to the possible and to the existing." Being an eternal truth, space must have its place in that which is simply the active unity of all eternal truths, — the mind of God. "Its truth and reality are based upon God. It is an order whose source is God." Since God is *purus actus*, he is the immediate, the efficient source only of that which partakes in some degree of his own nature, or is rational; and here is another clear point of distinction between space and extension, between time and duration.

But we must ask more in detail regarding their nature. Admitting that they are relations, ideal and prior to particular experiences, the question must be asked, What sort of relations are they; how are they connected with the purely spiritual on one hand, and with the phenomenal on the other? Leibniz's most extended answers to these questions are given in his controversy with Clarke. The latter took much the same position regarding the nature of space (though not, indeed, concerning the origin of its idea) as Locke, and the arguments which Leibniz uses against him he might also have used, for the most part, against Locke. Locke and Clarke both conceived of space and time as wholly without intrinsic relation to objects and events. It is especially against this position that Leibniz argues, holding that space and time are simply orders or relations of objects and events, that space exists only where objects are existing, and that it is the order of their co-existence, or of their possible co-existence; while time exists only as events are occurring, and is the relation of their succession. Clarke, on the other hand, speaks of the universe of objects as bounded by and moving about in an empty space, and says that time existed before God created the finite world, so that the world came into a time already there to receive its on-goings, just as it fell into a space already there to receive its co-existences.

To get at the ideas of Leibniz, therefore, we cannot do better than follow the course of this discussion. He begins by saying that both space and time are purely relative, one being the order of co-existences, the other of successions. Space characterizes in terms of possibility an order of things existing at the same time, so far as they exist in mutual relations (*ensemble*), without regard to their special modes of existence. As to the alternate doctrine that space is a substance, or something absolute, it contradicts the principle of sufficient reason. Were space something absolutely uniform, without things placed in it, there would be no difference between one part and another, and it would be a matter of utter indifference to God why he gave bodies certain positions in space rather than others; similarly it would be a matter of indifference why he created the world when he did, if time were something independent of events. In other words, the supposed absoluteness of space and time would render the action of God wholly without reason, capricious, and at haphazard. Similarly, it contradicts the principle of "indiscernibles," by which Leibniz means the principle of specification, or distinction. According to him, to suppose two things exactly alike, is simply to imagine the same thing twice. Absolute uniformity, wholly undifferentiated, is a fiction impossible to realize in thought.

"Space considered without objects has nothing in it to determine it; it is accordingly nothing actual. The parts of space must be determined and distinguished by the objects which are in them." Finally, were space and time absolutely real things in themselves, they would be independent of God, and even limitations upon him. "They would be more substantial than substances. God would not be able to change or destroy them. They would be immutable and eternal in every part. Thus there would be an infinity of eternal things (these parts) independent of God." They would limit God because he would be obliged to exist *in* them. Only by existing through this independent time would he be eternal; only by extending through this independent space would he be omnipresent. Space and time thus become gods themselves.

When Clarke declares that by the absoluteness of space and time he does not mean that they are themselves substances, but only properties, attributes of substance, Leibniz advances the same arguments in different form. If space were the property of the things that are in space, it would belong now to one substance, now to another, and when empty of all material substance, even to an immaterial substance, perhaps to God. "Truly a strange attribute which is handed about from one thing to another. Substances thus leave their accidents as if they were old clothes, and other substances put them on." Since these finite spaces are in infinite space, and the latter is an attribute of God, it must be that an attribute of God is composed of parts, some of them empty, some full, some round, some square. So, too, whatever is in time would help make one of the attributes of God. "Truly a strange God," says Leibniz, "this Deity of parts" (*ce Dieu à parties*). Clarke's reply to this was that space and time are attributes of God and of God alone, not of things in space and time,—that, indeed, strictly speaking, there are no parts in space or in time; they are absolutely one. This was virtually to give up the whole matter. It was to deny the existence of finite spaces and times, and to resolve them into an indefinite attribute of God. Such a view, as Leibniz points out, not only is contrary to experience, but affords no aid in determining the actual concrete forms and situations of bodies, and durations and successions of events. The absolute space and time, having no parts, are wholly out of relations to these concrete existences. The latter require, therefore, a space and a time that are relations or orders. Clarke's hypothesis is, as Leibniz says, wholly without use or function, and requires a theory like that of Leibniz to account for the actually determinate forms of experience. In his last reply Clarke shifts his ground again, and says that space and time are *effects* of God's existence; "they are the necessary results of his existence." "His existence is the cause of space and time." The death of Leibniz prevented any further reply. It is not hard to imagine, however, that in a general way his reply would have been to ask how space and time are at once attributes essential and necessary to God, as constituting his immensity and eternity, and effects dependent upon his existence. To take this latter position, indeed, seems to abandon the position that they are absolute, and to admit that, like the rest of God's creation, they are relative and finite.

So much for Leibniz's polemic. Its meaning is that space and time have significance only with reference to things and events, that they are the intellectual, the ideal side of these objects and occurrences, being the relations which give them order and unity. A space which is not the space of objects, which is not space in and through objects, is an inanity; it is not spirit, it is not matter; it is not a relation of either. It is nothingness magnified to infinity, and then erected into existence. And all for nothing; for it does not enable us to account for a single concrete fact of experience. For this we must have recourse to relations and orders of existence. Space is therefore to be defined as the order which makes it possible for objects to have situation; time as that which makes it possible for events to have dating, — not as if they were actually prior to them, and although nothings in themselves, yet capable of giving concrete determination to things, but as *actually* the relations themselves, and as *ideally* necessary for the coherent experience of co-existent objects and of connected events. As Leibniz puts it epigrammatically: "Space is the order of possible constants; time the order of inconstant possibilities."

We have finished the exposition of the views of Leibniz about matter and material facts. One question, however, remains to be discussed, — a question which Leibniz's contemporary critics would not allow him to pass over in silence, even had he been so disposed. What is the reality of matter, of motion, of space, and of time? Since they are, as Leibniz says, only phenomena, not absolute realities, what distinguishes them from dreams, from illusions? What distinguishes sensible phenomena from capricious fantasies, and gives them reality?

Leibniz begins his answer by pointing out that the mere fact that bodies are phenomena does not make them unreal. To say that anything is phenomenal is to say that it is sensible; but "the senses make no declaration regarding metaphysical matters" such as truth and reality. The senses, in a word, only inform us that the experiences are there for the senses, that they are sensible. What is the ultimate nature of the sensible or the phenomenal, what is their reality, is a question wholly outside the province of sense. The questions of ultimate nature, of reality, are questions of metaphysics, and hence are to be decided by the reason, not by the senses. And Leibniz goes on to say that the truthfulness of the senses, since it concerns only the sensible, consists in the reciprocal agreement of sensible facts, and in that we are not deceived in reasoning from one to another. An isolated sense-experience could not be said to be either true or false, real or illusory. It would be true that it was experienced, and that is all that could be said about it. But since our experiences are not thus separated, but have a certain order, there arises what we may call sensible reality and illusion. When the order between two facts remains the same "in different times and places and in the experience of different men," we call these facts real. If, however, our experience cannot be repeated by ourselves or by other men when the same conditions (that is, connections) are present, it is unreal, or false. It is thus "the *relation* of phenomena which guarantees truth of fact regarding sensible objects." Constancy, regularity, justify us in ascribing reality; chaotic change and lack of orderly connection are a sign of unreality. Even our dreams have a reality; for they have their connections and place in experience. If we understood their connections we should even be able to explain their apparent lack of connection with the rest of experience. Leibniz thinks that both the Academicians and Sceptics and their opponents erred in attempting to find greater reality in sensible things than that of regular phenomena. Since our observations and judgments upon sensible phenomena are of such a nature that we can predict future phenomena and prepare for them, we have all the reality in them that can be had or asked for. Even if it be granted possible (as it must be on this basis) that, metaphysically speaking, sense-experience is only a connected dream, it yet has a sufficient reality; for we are not deceived in the measures taken with reference to phenomena, provided that we act on the ground of their observed harmonies and relations. Thus while we are obliged to admit that our senses inform us that there are hard, passive, extended, indivisible things, not perfectly continuous and not intellectual in their nature, and we know on metaphysical grounds that this information is not correct, we cannot say that our senses deceive us, for sense makes no statements regarding such matters. It is our reason that errs if it takes the information that the senses give as if it were a declaration of reason itself. Sensible things have all the reality necessary for this range of experience, — *practical*, — such regularity of co-existence and sequence as allows us to act without being led astray.

But if we regard sense-phenomena not merely in their connection with one another, but in their dependence upon the absolute realities, we have still better justification for their comparative reality. These phenomena are consequences of necessary and eternal truths. One endowed with a perfect knowledge of such truths would be able to deduce, *à priori*, the phenomena from them. The reality of sensible phenomena thus consists not merely in their connection with one another, but in the fact that they are connected as the laws of the intelligible world require. They follow not only rules of co-existence and sequence; but these rules may be brought under general laws of motion, which in turn may be deduced from geometrical principles. These latter, however, are *a priori*; they are truths which are grounded in the very intelligence of God. The sensible has its basis in the ideal. To state the same fact in another way, all sensible phenomena occur in time and space; or rather, time and space are the orders, the relations, of phenomena occurring and existing. But, as we have just seen, time and space are ideal. A relation, as Leibniz points out, being neither attribute nor accident, cannot be *in* the things which it relates, as their possession. In his own words, it cannot be conceived as if it had one leg in one object, the other leg in the other. A relation is not a material bond, running through or cementing objects; it is ideal, existing in the mind. And while it is true that space and time are the relations of objects and events, it is also true that if all objects and events were annihilated, space and time would continue to have their ideal existence in the intelligence of God as the eternal conditions of phenomena. They thus form the links between absolute reality and the reality of sensible existence. The principle of sufficient reason forms another link. It may be recalled that in discussing Leibniz's theory of volition we found that the will of God in relation to the sensible world is always determined by the choice of the better; that in this consists the controlling reason and regulative principle of all that occurs and exists. Thus for every fact in the sensible world there is connection with "metaphysical," or absolute, reality, not only through the medium of the intellectual relations of time and space, but through the dynamic intermediary of the divine will acting in accordance with the divine reason. Sensible facts have, then, a reality, but a dependent one. There would be no *contradiction* involved if they were not what they actually are.

We may sum up the matter by saying that the reality of sensible phenomena consists in the constancy of the mutual order in which they exist, and in the dependence of this order upon the divine Intelligence and Will. In this respect, at least, Leibniz resembles the young Irish idealist, Berkeley, who only seven years after Leibniz wrote the "New Essays" composed his "Principles of Human Knowledge," urging that the immediate reality of sense-phenomena consists in their "steadiness, order, and coherence," "in a constant uniform working," and that this "gives us a foresight which enables us to regulate our actions for the benefit of life." It was Berkeley also who wrote that their ultimate reality consists in their being ideas of a Divine Spirit. This was six years before the death of Leibniz. Yet it does not appear that Berkeley knew of Leibniz, and the only allusion to Berkeley which I have found in the writings of Leibniz shows that Leibniz knew only of that caricature of his views which has always been current, — that Berkeley was one who denied the existence of any external world. What he writes is as follows: "As for him in Ireland who questions the reality of 'bodies,' he seems neither to offer what is rational, nor sufficiently to explain his own ideas. I suspect that he is one of those men who are desirous of making themselves known through paradoxes."

CHAPTER IX.

SOME FUNDAMENTAL CONCEPTIONS.

THE fundamental category of Locke, as of all who take simply a mechanical view of experience, is that of substance. He had good reason to be surprised when the Bishop of Worcester objected that Locke wished "to discard substance out of the world." How can that be so, Locke asks, when I say that "our idea of body is an extended solid substance, and our idea of soul is of a substance that thinks." And he adds, "Nay, as long as there is any simple idea or sensible quality left, according to my way of arguing, substance cannot be discarded." Everything that really exists, is, according to Locke, substance. But substance to Locke, as again to all who interpret the universe after sensible categories, is unknowable. For such categories allow only of external relations; they admit only of static existence. Substance, in this way of looking at it, must be distinct from its qualities, and must be simply the existing substratum in which they inhere.

Locke's account of the way in which we get the idea, and of its nature, is as follows: "All the ideas of all the sensible qualities of a cherry come into my mind by sensation. The ideas of these qualities and actions, or powers, are perceived by the mind to be by themselves inconsistent with existence. They cannot subsist of themselves. Hence the mind perceives their necessary connection with inherence, or with being supported." Correlative to the idea of being supported is, of course, the idea of the support. But this idea "is not represented to the mind by any clear and distinct idea; the obscure and vague, indistinct idea of thing or something, is all that is left." Or yet more simply, "Taking notice that a certain number of simple ideas go together, and not imagining how these simple ideas can subsist by themselves, we accustom ourselves to suppose some substratum wherein they do subsist, and from which they do result." Hence the only idea we have of it is of something which underlies known qualities. It is their "supposed, but unknown, support."

If we translate these expressions into the ideas of to-day, we see that they are equivalent to the view of the world which is given us by scientific categories when these categories are regarded not merely as scientific, but also as philosophic; that is, capable of interpreting and expressing the ultimate nature of experience. This modern view uses the words "things-in-themselves" (or absolute realities) and "phenomena." It says that we know nothing of existence as it is in itself, but only of its phenomena. Mind, matter, objects, are all substances, all equally substances, and all have their unknown essence and their phenomenal appearance. Such a distinction between the known and the unknown can rest, it is evident, only upon a separation between reality and phenomena similar to that which Locke makes between substance and qualities. In knowing the latter, we know nothing of the former. Although the latter are called "phenomena," they do not really manifest the substantial reality; they conceal it. This absolute distinction between substance and quality, between reality and phenomenon, rests, in turn, upon the hypothesis that reality is *mere* existence; that is, it is something which is, and that is all. It is a substratum; it lies under, in a passive way, qualities; it is (literally) substance; it simply stands, inactively, under phenomena. It may, by possibility, *have* actions; but it *has* them. Activities are qualities which, like all qualities, are in external relation to the substance. Being, in other words, is the primary notion, and "being" means something essentially passive and merely enduring, accidentally and secondarily something acting. Here, as elsewhere, Locke is the father of the mechanical philosophy of to-day.

We have already learned how completely Leibniz reverses this way of regarding reality. According to Locke, reality essentially is; and in its being there is no ground of revelation of itself. It then acts; but these actions, "powers, or qualities," since not flowing from the very being of substance, give no glimpse into its true nature. According to Leibniz, reality acts, and *therefore* is. Its being is conditioned upon its activity. It is not first there, and secondly acts; but its "being there" is its activity. Since its very substance is activity, it is impossible that it should not manifest its true nature. Its every activity is a revelation of itself. It cannot hide itself as a passive subsistence behind qualities or phenomena. It must break forth into them. On the other hand, since the qualities are not something which merely inhere in an underlying support, but are the various forms or modes of the activity which constitutes reality, they necessarily reveal it. They *are* its revelations. There is here no need to dwell further on the original dynamic nature of substance; what was said in the way of general exposition suffices. It is only in its relations to Locke's view as just laid down that it now concerns us.

In the first place, Leibniz points out that qualities are "abstract," while substance is "concrete." The qualities, from the very fact that they have no self-subsistence, are only relations, while the substance, as that of which they are qualities, or from which they are abstractions, is concrete. It is, Leibniz says, to invert the true order to take qualities or abstract terms as the best known and most easily comprehended, and "concretes" as unknown, and as having the most difficulty about them. "It is abstractions which give birth to almost all our difficulties," and Locke's error here is that he begins with abstractions, and takes them to be most open to intelligence. Locke's second error is separating so completely substance and attribute. "After having distinguished," says Leibniz, "two things in substance, the attributes or predicates, and the common subject of these predicates, it is not to be wondered at that we cannot conceive anything in particular in the subject. This result is necessary, since we have separated all the attributes in which there is anything definite to be conceived. Hence to demand anything more than a mere unknown somewhat in the subject, is to contradict the supposition which was made in making the abstraction and in conceiving separately the subject and its qualities or accidents." We are indeed ignorant of a subject from which abstraction has been made of all defining and characteristic qualities; "but this ignorance results from our demanding a sort of knowledge of which the object does not permit." In short, it is a credit to our knowledge, not an aspersion upon it, that we cannot know that which is thoroughly unreal, — a substance deprived of all attributes. This is, indeed, a remark which is applicable to the supposed unknowableness of pure Being, or Absolute Being, when it is defined as the absence of all relations (as is done, for example, by Mr. Spencer to-day).

Closely connected with the notion of substance are the categories of identity and diversity. These relations are of course to Locke thoroughly external. It is "relation of time and place which always determines identity." "That that had one beginning is the same thing; and that which had a different beginning in time and place from that, is not the same, but diverse." It is therefore easy to discover the principle of individuation. It "is existence itself, which determines a being of any sort to a particular time and place, incommunicable to two beings of the same kind." He applies this notion to organic being, including man, and to the personal identity of man. The identity of an organism, vegetable, brute, or human, is its continuous organization; "it is the participation of the same continued life, by constantly fleeting particles of matter in succession vitally united to the same organized body." *Personal* identity is constituted by a similar continuity of consciousness. "It being the same consciousness that makes a man be himself to himself, personal identity depends on that only." It "consists not in the identity of substance, but in the identity of consciousness." It will be noticed that Locke uses the notion of identity which he has already established to explain organic and personal unity. It is the "*same* continued life," "*identity* of consciousness," that constitute them. We are, hence, introduced to no new principle. Identity is even in personality a matter of temporal and spatial relations.

In the general account of the system of Leibniz it was pointed out that it is characteristic of his thought to regard identity and distinction as internal principles, and as necessarily implied in each other. We need not go over that ground again, but simply see how he states his position with reference to what is quoted from Locke. These are his words: "Besides the difference of place and time there is always necessary an *internal principle* [or law] of distinction, so that while there may be several things of the same species, there are no two things exactly alike. Thus, although time and place (that is, relations to the external) aid us in distinguishing things, things do not cease to be distinguished in themselves. The essence of identity and diversity does not consist in time and place, although it is true that diversity of things is accompanied with that of time and place, since they carry along with them different impressions upon the thing;" that is, they expose the thing to different surroundings. But in reality "it is things which diversify times and places from one another, for in themselves these are perfectly similar, not being substances or complete realities."

The principle of individuation follows, of course, from this. "If two individuals were perfectly similar and equal, that is, indistinguishable in themselves, there would be no principle of individuation; there would not be two individuals." Thus Leibniz states his important principle of the "identity of indiscernibles," the principle that where there is not some internal differentiating principle which specifies the existence in this or that definite way, there is no individual. Leibniz here states, in effect, the principle of organic unity, the notion that concrete unity is a unity *of* differences, not *from* them. It is the principle which allows him at once to accept and transform the thought of Spinoza that all qualification or determination is negation. Spinoza, in spite of his intellectual greatness, conceived of distinction or determination as external, and hence as external negation. But since ultimate reality admits of no external negation, it must be without distinction, an all-inclusive one. But to Leibniz the negation is internal; it is determination of its own being into the greatest possible riches. "Things that are conceived as absolutely uniform and containing no variety are pure abstractions." "Things indistinguishable in themselves, and capable of being distinguished only by external characteristics without internal foundation, are contrary to the most important principles of reason. The truth is that every being is capable of change [or differentiation], and is itself actually changed in such a way that in itself it differs from every other."

As to organic bodies, so far as they *are* bodies, or corporeal, they are one and identical only in appearance. "They are not the same an instant. . . . Bodies are in constant flux." "They are like a river which is always changing its water, or like the ship of Theseus which the Athenians are constantly repairing." Such unity as they really possess is like all unity, — ideal or spiritual. "They remain the same individual by virtue of that same soul or spirit which constitutes the 'Ego' in those individuals who think." "Except for the soul, there is neither the same life nor any vital union." As to personal identity, Leibniz distinguishes between "physical or real" identity and "moral." In neither case, however, is it a unity which excludes plurality, an identity which does not comprehend diversity. "Every spirit has," he says, "traces of all the impressions which it has ever experienced, and even presentiments of all that ever will happen. But these feelings are generally too minute to be distinguished and brought into consciousness, though they may be sometime developed. This *continuity* and *connection* of *perceptions* makes up the real identity of the individual, while *apperceptions* (that which is consciously apprehended of past experiences) constitute the moral identity and make manifest the real identity." We have had occasion before to allude to the part played in the Leibnizian philosophy by "minute perceptions" or "unconscious ideas." Of them he says, relative to the present point, that "insensible perceptions mark and even constitute the sameness of the individual, which is characterized by the residua preserved from its preceding states, as they form its connection with its present state." If these connections are "apperceived" or brought into distinct consciousness, there is moral identity as well. As he expresses it in one place: "The self (*soi*) is real and physical identity; the appearance of self, accompanied with truth, is personal identity." But the essential point in either case is that the identity is not that of a substance underlying modifications, nor of a consciousness which merely accompanies all mental states, but is the connection, the active continuity, or — in Kant's word — the synthesis, of all particular forms of the mental life. The self is not the most abstract unity of experience, it is the most organic. What Leibniz says of his monads generally is especially true of the higher monads, — human souls. "They vary, up to infinity itself, with the greatest abundance, order, and beauty imaginable." Not a mathematical point, but life, is the type of Leibniz's conception of identity.

In the order in which Locke takes up his topics (and in which Leibniz follows him) we have omitted one subject, which, however, may find its natural place in the present connection, — the subject of infinity. In Locke's conception, the infinite is only a ceaseless extension or multiplication of the finite. He considers the topic immediately after the discussions of space, time, and number, and with good logic from his standpoint; for "finite and infinite," he says, are "looked upon by the mind as the modes of *quantity*, and are attributed, in their first designation, only to those things which have parts and are capable of increase and diminution." This is true even of the application of the term "infinite" to God, so far as concerns the attributes of duration and ubiquity; and as applied to his other attributes the term is figurative, signifying that they are incomprehensible and inexhaustible. Such being the idea of the infinite, it is attained as follows: There is no difficulty, says Locke, as to the way in which we come by the idea of the finite. Every obvious portion of extension and period of succession which affects us is bounded. If we take one of these periods or portions, we find that we can double it, or "otherwise multiply it," as often as we wish, and that there is no reason to stop, nor are we one jot nearer the end at any point of the multiplication than when we set out. "By repeating as often as we will any idea of space, we get the idea of infinity; by being able to repeat the idea of any length of duration, we come by the idea of eternity." There is a difference, then, between the ideas of the infinity of space, time, and number, and of an infinite space, time, and number. The former idea we have; it is the idea that we can continue without end the process of multiplication or progression. The latter we have not; it would be the idea of having completed the infinite multiplication, it would be the result of the never-ending progression. And this is evidently a contradiction in terms. To sum the matter up, the term "infinite" always relates to the notion of quantity. Quantity is that which is essentially capable of increase or decrease. There is then an infinity of quantity; there is no quantity which is the absolute limit to quantity. Such a quantity would be incapable of increase, and hence contradictory to quantity. But an actual infinite quantity (whether of space, time, or number) would be one than which there could be no greater; and hence the impossibility of our having a positive idea of an actual or completed infinite.

Leibniz's reply consists simply in carrying out this same thought somewhat further. It is granted that the idea of an infinite quantity of any kind is absurd and self-contradictory. But what does this prove, except that the notions of quantity and infinity are incompatible with each other, that they contradict each other? Hence, instead of the infinite being a mode of quantity, it must be conceived as essentially distinct from and even opposed to quantity. Locke's argument is virtually a *reductio ad absurdum* of the notion that the infinite is capable of parts. In the few pages of comment which Leibniz in 1696 wrote upon Locke, this topic of the infinite is one of the few touched upon. His words upon that occasion were as follows: "I agree with Mr. Locke that, properly speaking, there is no space, time, nor number which is infinite; and that it is only true that however great be a space, a time, or a number, there is always another which is still greater, and this without end; and that, *therefore*, the infinite is not to be found in a whole made up of parts. But it does not cease to exist: it is found in the absolute, which is without parts, and of which compound things [phenomena in space and time, or facts which may be numbered] are only limitations. The positive infinite being nothing else than the absolute, it may be said that there is, in this sense, a positive idea of the infinite, and that it is anterior to the idea of the finite." In other words, while the infinite is to Locke an indefinite extension of the finite, which alone is positively "given," to Leibniz the infinite is the positive and real, and the finite is only in and by it. The finite is the negative.

Leibniz amplifies this thought upon other occasions, as in his present more extended examination. "There is no infinite number, line, or quantity, if they are taken as true wholes." "We deceive ourselves in trying to imagine an absolute space which should be an infinite whole, composed of parts. There is none such. It is an idea which implies contradiction; and all these 'infinites' and 'infinitesimals' are of use only in geometry, as imaginary roots are in algebra." That which is ordinarily called the infinite, that is, the quantitative infinite, is in reality only the indefinite. "We involve ourselves in difficulty when we talk about a series of numbers extending *to* infinity; we imagine a last term, an infinite number, or one infinitely little. But these are only fictions. All number is finite and assignable [that is, of a certain definite quantity]; every line is the same. 'Infinites' and 'infinitesimals' signify only quantities which can be taken as large or as small as one wishes, simply for the purpose of showing that there is no error which can be assigned. Or we are to understand by the infinitely little, the state of vanishing or commencing of a quantum after the analogy of a quantum already formed." On the other hand, the true infinite "is not an aggregate, nor a whole of parts; it is not clothed with magnitude, nor does it consist in number. . . . The Absolute alone, the indivisible infinite, has true unity, — I mean God." And as he sums up the matter: "The infinite, consisting of parts, is neither one nor a whole; it cannot be brought under any notion of the mind except that of quantity. Only the infinite without parts is one, and this is not a whole [of parts]: this infinite is God."

It cannot be admitted, however, that Locke has given a correct account of the origin of the notion of the quantitative infinite, or — to speak philosophically, and not after the use of terms convenient in mathematics — the indefinite. According to him, its origin is the mere empirical repeating of a sensuous datum of time and space. According to Leibniz, this repetition, however long continued, can give no idea beyond itself; it can never generate the idea that the process of repetition may be continued without a limit. Here, as elsewhere, he objects that experience cannot guarantee notions beyond the limits of experience. Locke's process of repetition could tell us that a number *had* been extended up to a given point; not that it could be extended without limit. The source of this latter idea must be found, therefore, where we find the origin of all extra-empirical notions, — in reason. "Its origin is the same as that of universal and necessary truths." It is not the empirical process of multiplying, but the fact that the *same reason* for multiplying always exists, that originates and guarantees the idea. "Take a straight line and prolong it in such a way that it is double the first. It is evident that the second, being perfectly *similar* to the first, can be itself doubled; and we have a third, which in turn is *similar* to the preceding. The *same reason* always being present, it is not possible that the process should ever be brought to a stop. Thus the line can be prolonged 'to infinity.' Therefore the idea of 'infinity' comes from the consideration of the identity of relation or of reason."

The considerations which we have grouped together in this chapter serve to show the fundamental philosophical difference between Locke and Leibniz. Although, taken in detail, they are self-explanatory, a few words may be permitted upon their unity and ultimate bearing. It is characteristic of Locke that he uses the same principle of explanation with reference to the conceptions of substance, identity and diversity, and infinity, and that this principle is that of spatial and temporal relation. Infinity is conceived as quantitative, as the successive addition of times and spaces; identity and diversity are oneness and difference of existence as determined by space and time; substance is the underlying static substratum of qualities, and, as such, is considered after the analogy of things existing in space and through time. It must not be forgotten that Locke believed as thoroughly as Leibniz in the substantial existence of the world, of the human soul, and of God; in the objective continuity of the world, and the personal identity of man, and in the true infinity of God. Whatever negative or sceptical inferences may have afterwards been drawn from Locke's premises were neither drawn nor dreamed of by him. His purpose was in essence one with that of Leibniz.

But the contention of Leibniz is that when substance, identity, and infinity are conceived of by mechanical categories, or measured by the sensible standard of space and time, they lose their meaning and their validity. According to him such notions are spiritual in their nature, and to be spiritually conceived of. "Spiritual," however, does not mean opposed to the sensible; it does not mean something to be known by a peculiar kind of intuition unlike our knowledge of anything else. It means the active and organic basis of the sensible, its significance and ideal purpose. It is known by knowing the sensible or mechanical as it really is; that is, as it is completely, as a *concretum*, in Leibniz's phrase. Leibniz saw clearly that to make the infinite something at one end of the finite, as its mere external limit, or something miraculously intercalated into the finite, was to deprive it of meaning, and, by making it unknowable, to open the way for its denial. To make identity consist in the removal of all diversity (as must be done if it be thought after the manner of external relations), is to reduce it to nothing, — as Hume, indeed, afterwards showed. Substance, which is merely a support behind qualities, is unknowable, and hence unverifiable. While, then, the aim of both Locke and Leibniz as regards these categories was the same, Leibniz saw what Locke did not, — that to interpret them after the manner of existence in space and time, to regard them (in Leibniz's terminology) as mathematical, and not as metaphysical, is to defeat that aim. The sole way to justify them, and in justifying them to give relative validity to the sensible and phenomenal, is to demonstrate their spiritual and dynamic nature, to show them as conditioning space and time, and not as conditioned by them.

CHAPTER X.

THE NATURE AND EXTENT OF KNOWLEDGE.

THE third book of Locke's Essay is upon words and language; and in the order of treatment this would be the next topic for discussion. But much of what is said in this connection both by Locke and by Leibniz is philological, rhetorical, and grammatical in character, and although not without interest in itself, is yet without any especial bearing upon the philosophical points in controversy. The only topics in this book demanding our attention are general and particular terms; but these fall most naturally into the discussion of general and particular knowledge. In fact, it is not the terms which Locke actually discusses, but the ideas for which the terms stand. We pass on accordingly, without further ceremony, to the fourth book, which is concerning knowledge in general. Locke defines knowledge as "nothing but the perception of the connection and agreement, or disagreement and repugnancy, of any of our ideas." These agreements or disagreements may be reduced to four sorts,— Identity, or diversity; Relation; Co-existence, or necessary connection; Real existence. The statement of identity and diversity is implied in all knowledge whatsoever. By them "the mind clearly and infallibly perceives each idea to agree with itself and be what it is, and all distinct ideas to disagree; *i. e.*, the one not to be the other." The agreement of relation is such knowledge as the mind derives from the *comparison* of its ideas. It includes mathematical knowledge. The connection of co-existence "belongs particularly to substances." Locke's example is that "gold is fixed," — by which we understand that the idea of fixedness goes along with that group of ideas which we call gold. All statements of fact coming under the natural sciences would fall into this class. The fourth sort is "that of actual and real existence agreeing to any idea."

Leibniz's criticism upon these statements of Locke is brief and to the point. He admits Locke's definition of knowledge, qualifying it, however, by the statement that in much of our knowledge, perhaps in all that is merely empirical, we do not know the reason and connection of things and hence cannot be said to *perceive* the agreement or disagreement of ideas, but only to feel it confusedly. His most important remark, however, is to the effect that relation is not a special kind of knowledge, but that all Locke's four kinds are varieties of relation. Locke's "connection" of ideas which makes knowledge is nothing but relation. And there are two kinds of relation, — those of "comparison" and of "concourse." That of comparison states the identity or distinction of ideas, either in whole or in part. That of concourse contains Locke's two classes of co-existence and existence. "When we say that a thing really exists, this existence is the predicate, — that is to say, a notion connected with the idea which is the subject; and there is connection between these two notions. The existence of an object of an idea may be considered as the concourse of this object with me. Hence comparison, which marks identity or diversity, and concourse of an object with me (or with the *ego*) are the only forms of knowledge."

Leibniz leaves the matter here; but he only needed to develop what is contained in this statement to anticipate Berkeley and Kant in some of the most important of their discoveries. The contradiction which lies concealed in Locke's account is between his definition of knowledge in general, and knowledge of real existence in particular. One is the agreement or disagreement of *ideas;* the other is the agreement of an idea *with an object.* Berkeley's work, in its simplest form, was to remove this inconsistency. He saw clearly that the "object" was an intruder here. If knowledge lies in the connection of *ideas*, it is impossible to get outside the ideas to find an object with which they agree. Either that object is entirely unknown, or it is an idea. It is impossible, therefore, to find the knowledge of reality in the comparison of an idea with an object. It must be in some property of the ideas themselves.

Kant developed more fully the nature of this property, which constitutes the "objectivity" of our ideas. It is their connection with one another according to certain *necessary* forms of perception and rules of conception. In other words, the reality of ideas lies in their being connected by the necessary and hence universal relations of synthetic intelligence, or, as Kant often states it, in their agreement with the conditions of self-consciousness. It is not, I believe, unduly stretching either the letter or the spirit of Leibniz to find in that "concourse of the object with the ego" which makes its reality, the analogue of this doctrine of Kant; it is at all events the recognition of the fact that reality is not to be found in the relating of ideas to unknown things, but in their relation to self-conscious intelligence. The points of similarity between Kant and Leibniz do not end here. Leibniz's two relations of "comparison" and "concourse" are certainly the congeners of Kant's "analytic" and "synthetic" judgments. But Leibniz, as we shall see hereafter, trusts too thoroughly to the merely formal relations of identity and contradiction to permit him such a development of these two kinds of relation as renders Kant's treatment of them epoch-making.

The discussion then advances to the subject of degrees of knowledge, of which Locke recognizes three, — intuitive, demonstrative, and sensitive. Intuitive knowledge is immediate knowledge, — recognition of likeness or difference without the intervention of a third idea; it is the most certain and clear of all knowledge. In demonstrative knowledge the agreement or disagreement cannot be perceived directly, because the ideas cannot be put together so as to show it. Hence the mind has recourse to intermediaries. "And this is what we call reasoning." Demonstrative rests on intuitive knowledge, because each intermediate idea used must be immediately perceived to be like or unlike its neighboring idea, or it would itself need intermediates for its proof. Besides these two degrees of knowledge there is "another perception of the mind employed about the particular existence of finite things without us, which, going beyond bare probability, and yet not reaching perfectly to either of the foregoing degrees of certainty, passes under the name of knowledge."

Leibniz's comments are again brief. The primitive truths which are known by intuition are to be divided into two classes, — truths of reason and of fact. The primitive truths of reason are necessary, and may be called identical, because they seem only to repeat the same thing, without teaching us anything. A is A. A is not non-A. Such propositions are not frivolous or useless, because the conclusions of logic are demonstrated by means of identical propositions, and many of those of geometry by the principle of contradiction. All the intuitive truths of reason may be said to be made known through the "immediation" of ideas. The intuitive truths of fact, on the other hand, are contingent and are made known through the "immediation" of feeling. In this latter class come such truths as the Cartesian, "I think, therefore I am." Neither class can be proved by anything more certain.

Demonstration is defined by Leibniz as by Locke. The former recognizes, however, two sorts, — analytic and synthetic. Synthesis goes from the simple to the complex. There are many cases, however, where this is not applicable; where it would be a task "equal to drinking up the sea to attempt to make all the necessary combinations. Here the method of exclusions should be employed, cutting off many of the useless combinations." If this cannot be done, then it is analysis which gives the clew into the labyrinth. He is also of the opinion that besides demonstration, giving certainty, there should be admitted an art of calculating probabilities, — the lack of which is, he says, a great defect in our present logic, and which would be more useful than a large part of our demonstrative sciences. As to sensitive knowledge, he agrees with Locke that there is such a thing as real knowledge of objects without us, and that this variety does not have the same metaphysical certainty as the other two; but he disagrees regarding its criterion. According to Locke, the criterion is simply the greater degree of vividness and force that sensations have as compared with imaginations, and the actual pleasures or pains which accompany them. Leibniz points out that this criterion, which in reality is purely emotional, is of no great value, and states the principle of the reality of sensible phenomena which we have already given, repeating that it is found in the *connection* of phenomena, and that "this connection is verified by means of the truths of reason, just as the phenomena of optics are explained by geometry."

The discussion regarding "primitive truths," axioms, and maxims, as well as the distinction between truths of fact and of reason, has its most important bearing in Locke's next chapter. This chapter has for its title the "Extent of Human Knowledge," and in connection with the sixth chapter, upon universal propositions, and with the seventh, upon axioms, really contains the gist of the treatment of knowledge. It is here also that are to be considered chapters three and six of book third, having respectively as their titles, "Of General Terms," and "Of the Names of Substances."

To understand Locke's views upon the extent and limitations of our knowledge, it is necessary to recur to his theory of its origin. If we compare what he says about the origin of ideas from sensations with what he says about the development of general knowledge from particular, we shall find that Locke unconsciously puts side by side two different, and even contradictory, theories upon this point. In the view already given when treating of sensation, knowledge originates from the combination, the addition, of the simple ideas furnished us by our senses. It begins with the simple, the unrelated, and advances to the complex. But according to the doctrine which he propounds in treating of general terms, knowledge begins with the individual, which is already qualified by definite relations, and hence complex, and proceeds, by abstracting some of these qualities, towards the simple. Or, in Locke's own language, "ideas become general by separating from them the circumstances of time and place and any other ideas that may *determine* them to this and that particular existence." And, still more definitely, he says that general ideas are framed by "leaving out of the *complex* idea of individuals that which is peculiar to each, and retaining only what is common to them all." From this it follows that "general and universal belong not to the real existence of things, but are the inventions and creatures of the understanding." "When we quit particulars, the generals that rest are only creatures of our own making. . . . The signification they have is nothing but a relation that by the mind of man is added to them." And in language which reminds us of Kant, but with very different bearing, he says that relations are the workmanship of the understanding. The abstract idea of what is common to all the members of the class constitutes "nominal essence." This nominal essence, not being a particular existence in nature, but the "workmanship of the understanding," is to be carefully distinguished from the real essence, "which is the being of anything whereby it is what it is." This real essence is evidently equivalent to the unknown "substance" of which we have heard before. "It is the real, internal, and unknown constitution of things." In simple or unrelated ideas and in modes the real and the nominal essence is the same; and hence whatever is demonstrated of one is demonstrated of the other. But as to substance it is different, the one being natural, the other artificial. The nominal essence always relates to sorts, or classes, and is a pattern or standard by which we classify objects. In the individual there is nothing essential, in this sense. "Particular beings, considered barely in themselves, will be found to have all their qualities equally essential to them, or, which is more, nothing at all." As for the "real essence" which things have, "we only suppose its being without precisely knowing what it is."

Locke here presents us with the confusion which, in one form or another, is always found in empiricism, and which indeed is essential to it. Locke, like the ordinary empiricist, has no doubt of the existence of real things. His starting-point is the existence of two substances, mind and matter; while, further, there is a great number of substances of each kind. Each mind and every separate portion of matter is a distinct substance. This supposed deliverance of common sense Locke never called into question. Working on this line, all knowledge will consist in abstraction from the ready-made things presented to us in perception, "in leaving out from the complex idea of individuals" something belonging to them. But on the other hand, Locke never doubts that knowledge begins with sensation, and that, therefore, the process of knowledge is one of adding simple, unrelated elements. The two theories are absolutely opposed to each other, and yet one and the same philosophical inference may be drawn from each; namely, that only the particular is real, and that the universal (or relations) is an artificial product, manufactured in one case by abstraction from the real individual, in the other by compounding the real sensation.

The result is, that when he comes to a discussion of the extent of knowledge, he admits knowledge of self, of God, and of "things," only by a denial of his very definition of knowledge, while knowledge of other conceptions, like those of mathematics, is not knowledge of reality, but only of ideas which we ourselves frame. All knowledge, that is to say, is obtained only either by contradicting his own fundamental notion, or by placing it in relations which are confessedly artificial and superinduced. It is to this point that we come.

The proposition which is fundamental to the discussion is that we have knowledge only where we perceive the agreement or disagreement of ideas. Locke then takes up each of his four classes of connection, in order to ascertain the extent of knowledge in it. Our knowledge of "identity and diversity extends as far as our ideas," because we intuitively perceive every idea to be "what it is, and different from any other." Locke afterwards states, however, that all purely identical propositions are "trifling," that is, they contain no instruction; they teach us nothing. Thus the first class of relations cannot be said to be of much avail. If we consider the fourth kind of knowledge, that of real existence, we have an intuitive knowledge of self, a demonstrative knowledge of God, and a sensitive knowledge of other things. But sensitive knowledge, it must be noted, "does not extend beyond the objects *actually present* to our senses." It can hardly be said, therefore, to assure us of the existence of *objects* at all. It only tells us what experiences are being at the time undergone. Furthermore, knowledge of all three (God, self, and matter), since of real being, and not of relations between ideas, contradicts his definition of knowledge. But perhaps we shall find knowledge more extended in the other classes. And indeed Locke tells us that knowledge of relations is the "largest field of our knowledge." It includes morals and mathematics; but it is to be noticed that, according to Locke, in both of these branches our demonstrations are not regarding facts, but regarding either "modes" framed by ourselves, or relations that are the creatures of our minds, — "extraneous and superinduced" upon the facts, as he says. He thus anticipates in substance, though not in phraseology, Hume's distinction between "matters of fact" and "connections of ideas," in the latter of which we may have knowledge, but not going beyond the combinations that we ourselves make.

This leaves one class, that of co-existence, to be examined. Here, if anywhere, must knowledge, worthy of being termed scientific, be found. This class, it will be remembered, comprehends our knowledge concerning substances. But this extends, according to Locke, "a very little way." The idea of a substance is a complex of various "simple ideas united in one subject and co-existing together." When we would know anything further concerning a substance, we only inquire what other simple ideas, besides those already united, co-exist with them. Since there is no *necessary* connection, however, among these simple ideas, since each is, by its very simplicity, essentially distinct from every other, or, as we have already learned, since nothing is essential to an individual, we can never be sure that any idea really co-exists with others. Or, as Locke says, in physical matters we "can go no further than particular experience informs us of. . . . We can have no certain knowledge of universal truths concerning natural bodies." And again, "universal propositions of whose truth and falsehood we have certain knowledge concern not existence;" while, on the other hand, "particular affirmations are only concerning existence, declaring only the *accidental* union or separation of ideas in things existing." This particular knowledge, it must be recalled, is, in turn, only sensitive, and thus extends not beyond the time when the sensation is had.

We are not surprised then at learning from Locke that regarding bodies "we are not capable of scientific knowledge." "Natural philosophy is not capable of being made a science;" or, as Locke elsewhere states it, knowledge regarding the nominal essence is "trifling" (Kant's analytic judgment); regarding the real essence is impossible. For example, when we say that all gold is fusible, this means either simply that fusibility is one of the ideas which we combine to get the general idea of gold, so that in making the given judgment we only expand our own notion; or it means that the "real" substance gold is always fusible. But this is a statement we have no right to make, and for two reasons: we do not know what the real substance gold is; and even if we did, we should not know that fusibility *always* co-exists with it. The summary of the whole matter is that "general certainty is to be found only in our ideas. Whenever we go to seek it elsewhere, in experiment or observations without us, our knowledge goes not beyond particulars."

It has been necessary to give an account of Locke's views at this length because it is in his discussion of the limitations and extent of knowledge that his theory culminates. While not working out his sensationalism as consistently as did Hume, he yet reduces knowledge to that of the existence of God and ourselves (whose natures, however, are unknown), and to a knowledge of mathematical and moral relations, which, however, concerns only "the habitudes and relations of abstract ideas." We have now to see by what means Leibniz finds a wider sphere for certain and general knowledge by his theory of intellectualism than Locke can by his sensationalism.

Leibniz's theory of knowledge rests upon a distinction between truths of fact, which are *a posteriori* and contingent, and truths of reason, which are *a priori* and necessary. In discussing his views regarding experience, we learned that, according to him, all judgments which are empirical are also particular, not allowing any inference beyond the given cases experienced. Experience gives only instances, not principles. If we postpone for the present the discussions of truths of reason, by admitting that they may properly be said to be at once certain and universal, the question arises how in matters of fact there can be any knowledge beyond that which Locke admits; and the answer is, that so far as the mere existence and occurrence of these facts is concerned, there is neither demonstrative nor general knowledge. But the intelligence of man does not stop with the isolated fact; it proceeds to inquire into its cause, to ascertain its conditions, and thus to see into, not merely its actual existence, but its *possibility*. In Leibniz's language: "The real existence of things that are not necessary is a point of fact or history; but the knowledge of possibilities or necessities (the necessary being that whose opposite is not possible) constitutes demonstrative science." In other words, it is the principle of causality, which makes us see a fact not as a mere fact, but as a dependent consequence; which elevates knowledge, otherwise contingent and particular, into the realm of the universal and apodictic. Underlying all "accidental union" is the real synthesis of causation.

If we follow the discussion as it centres about the terms "nominal" and "real," it stands as follows: Leibniz objects to the use of the term "essence" in this connection, but is willing to accept that of "definition;" for, as he says, a substance can have but one essence, while there may be several definitions, which, however, all express the same essence. The essence is the *possibility* of that which is under consideration; the definition is the statement of that which is supposed to be possible. The "nominal" definition, however, while it implies this possibility, does not expressly affirm it, — that is to say, it may always be doubted whether the nominal definition has any possibility (or reality) corresponding to it until experience comes to our aid and makes us know it *a posteriori*. A "real" definition, on the other hand, makes us know *a priori* the reality of the thing defined by showing us the mode of its production, "by exhibiting its cause or generation." Even our knowledge of facts of experience cannot be said, therefore, to be arbitrary, for we do not combine ideas just as we please, but "our combinations may be justified by reason which shows them to be possible, or by experience which shows them to be actual, and consequently also possible." To take Locke's example about gold, "the essence of gold is that which constitutes it and gives it its sensible qualities, and these qualities, so far as they enable us to recognize it, constitute its nominal essence, while a real and causal definition would enable us to explain the contexture or internal disposition. The nominal definition, however, is also real in one sense, — not in itself, indeed, since it does not enable us to know *a priori* the possibility or production of the body, but empirically real."

It is evident from these quotations that what Leibniz understands by "possibility" is the condition or cause of a given fact; and that, while Locke distinguishes between particular, accidental and demonstrative, general knowledge as two opposed kinds, concerned with two distinct and mutually exclusive spheres, with Leibniz they are distinctions in the aspect of the same sphere of fact. In reality there is no combination of qualities accidental, as Locke thought that by far the greater part were; in every empirical fact there is a cause or condition involved that is invariable, and that constitutes the reason of the fact. The "accidental" is only in the relation of our ideas to objects, not in the objects themselves. There may be accidental mental associations; there are no accidental relations. In empirical, or *a posteriori*, knowledge, so-called, the reason is there, but is not known. *A priori* knowledge, the real definition, discovers and explicitly states this reason. Contingent knowledge is therefore potentially rational; demonstrative knowledge is the actual development of the reasons implicitly contained in experience.

We may with advantage connect this discussion

with the fundamental doctrine of Locke and Leibniz regarding intelligence and reality. To Locke, as we have seen, knowledge is essentially a matter of relations or connections; but relations are "superinduced" and "extraneous" as regards the facts. Every act of knowledge constitutes, therefore, in some way a departure from the reality to be known. Knowledge and fact are, by their very definition, opposed to one another. But in Leibniz's view intelligence, or reason, enters into the constitution of reality; indeed, it is reality. The relations which are the "creatures of the understanding" are, therefore, not foreign to the material to be known, but are organic to it, forming its content. The process, then, in which the mind perceives the connections or relations of ideas or objects, is simply the process by which the mind comes to the consciousness of the real nature of these objects, not a process of "superinducing" unreal ideas upon them. The difficulty of Locke is the difficulty of every theory of knowledge that does not admit an organic unity of the knowing mind and the known universe. The theory is obliged to admit that all knowledge is in the form of relations which have their source in intelligence. But being tied to the view that reality is distinct from intelligence, it is obliged to draw the conclusion that these relations are not to be found in actual existence, and hence that all knowledge, whatever else it may be, is unreal in the sense that it does not and cannot conform to actual fact. But, in the theory of Leibniz, the process of relating which is the essence of knowledge is only the realization on the part of the individual mind of the relations or reasons that eternally constitute reality. Since reality is, and is what it is, through intelligence, whatever relations intelligence rightly perceives are not "extraneous" to reality, but are its "essence." As Leibniz says, "Truth consists in the relations between the objects of our ideas. This does not depend upon language, but is common to us with God, so that when God manifests a truth to us, *we acquire what is already in his understanding*. For although there is an infinite difference between his ideas and ours as to their perfection and extent, yet it is always true that as to the same relation they are identical. And it is in this relation that truth exists." To this may be added another statement, which throws still further light on this point: "Ideas are eternally in God, and are in us before we perceive them."

We have now to consider somewhat more in detail the means by which the transformation of empirical into rational knowledge is carried on. Leibniz points out that the difficulty concerning scientific knowledge of sensible facts is not lack of data, but, in a certain sense, superfluity of data. It is not that we perceive no connections among objects, but that we perceive many which we cannot reduce to one another. "Our experiences," says Leibniz, "are simple only in appearance, for they are always accompanied by circumstances connected with them, although these relations are not understood by us. These circumstances furnish material capable of explanation and analysis. There is thus a sort of *pleonasm* in our perceptions of sensible objects and qualities, since we have more than one idea of the same object. Gold can be nominally defined in many ways. Such definitions are only *provisional.*" This is to say, empirical knowledge will become rational when it is possible to view any subject-matter as a unity, instead of a multiplicity of varied aspects. And on this same subject he says, in another connection: "A great number of experiences can furnish us data more than sufficient for scientific knowledge, provided only we have the art of using these data." The aim of science is therefore, to discover the dynamic unity which makes a whole of what appears to be a mere mass of accidentally connected circumstances. This unity of relations is the individual.

It is thus evident that to Leibniz the individual is not the beginning of knowledge, but its goal. The individual is the organic, the dynamic unity of the variety of phases or notions presented us in sense-experience. Individuality is not "simplicity" in the sense of Locke; that is, separation from all relations. It is complete connection of all relations. "It is impossible for us to have [complete] knowledge of individuals, and to find the means of determining exactly the individuality of anything; for in individuality all circumstances are combined. Individuality envelops the infinite. Only so far as we know the infinite do we know the individual, on account of the influence (if this word be correctly understood) that all things in the universe exercise upon one another." Leibniz, in short, remains true to his conception of the monad as the ultimate reality; for the monad, though an individual, yet has the universe as its content. We shall be able, therefore, to render our sensible experiences rational just in the degree in which we can discover the underlying relations and dependencies which make them members of one individual.

For the process of transformation Leibniz relies especially upon two methods,—those of mathematics and of classification. Of the former he here says but little; but the entire progress of physical science since the time of Leibniz has been the justification of that little. In the passage already quoted regarding the need of method for using our sensible data, he goes on to say that the "infinitesimal analysis has given us the means of allying physics and geometry, and that dynamics has furnished us with the key to the general laws of nature." It is certainly competent testimony to the truth of Leibniz's fundamental principles that he foresaw also the course which the development of biological science would take. No classification based upon resemblances, says Leibniz in effect, can be regarded as wholly arbitrary, since resemblances are found in nature also. The only question is whether our classification is based upon superficial or fundamental identities; the superficial resemblances being such as are external, or the effects of some common cause, while the fundamental resemblances are such as are the cause of whatever other similarities are found. "It can be said that whatever we compare or distinguish with truth, nature differentiates, or makes agree, also; but that nature has differences and identities which are better than ours, which we do not know. . . . *The more we discover the generation of species*, and the more we follow in our classifications the conditions that are required for their production, the nearer we approach the natural order." Our classifications, then, so far as they depend upon what is conditioned, are imperfect and provisional, although they cannot be said to be false (since "while nature may give us those more complete and convenient, it will not give the lie to those we have already"); while so far as they rest upon what is causal and conditioning, they are true, general, and necessary. In thus insisting that classification should be genetic, Leibniz anticipated the great service which the theory of evolution has done for biological science in enabling science to form classes which are "natural;" that is, based on identity of origin.

Leibniz culminates his discussion of classification as a method of translating the empirical into the rational, by pointing out that it rests upon the law of continuity; and that this law contains two factors, — one equivalent to the axiom of the Realists, that nature is nowhere empty; the other, to that of the Nominalists, that nature does nothing uselessly. "One of these principles seems to make nature a prodigal, the other a miser; and yet both are true if properly understood," says Leibniz. "Nature is like a good manager, sparing where it is necessary, in order to be magnificent. It is magnificent in its effects, and economical in the causes used to produce them." In other words, classification becomes science when it presents us with both unity and difference. The principle of unity is that of nature as a miser and economical; that of differentiation is the principle of nature as prodigal and magnificent. The thoroughly differentiated unity is nature as self-specifying, or as an organic, not an abstract, unity.

The gist of the whole matter is, then, that experience presents us with an infinity of ideas, which may appear at first sight arbitrary and accidental in their connections. This appearance, however, is not the fact. These ideas are the effects of certain causes; and in ascertaining these conditions, we reduce the apparently unrelated variety of experiences to underlying unities, and these unities, like all real unities or simple beings, are spiritual and rational in nature. Leibniz's ordinary way of stating this is that the principle of truths of fact is that of *sufficient reason.* This principle Leibniz always treats as distinguished from that of identity (and contradiction) as the ruling category of truths of reason. And we shall follow him in discussing the two together.

"Our reasonings are based on two leading principles, — that of contradiction, in virtue of which we judge false all which contains contradiction, and true that which is opposed or contradictory to that which is false; and that of sufficient reason, in virtue of which we judge that no fact is true or actual, no proposition veritable, unless there is a sufficient reason why it is as it is, and not otherwise, although these reasons are generally unknown to us. Thus there are two sorts of truths, — those of reason, and those of fact. The truths of reason are necessary, and their opposites impossible; while those of fact are contingent, and their opposites possible. When a truth is necessary, its reason can be discovered by analysis, resolving it into ideas and truths that are simpler, until the primitive truths are arrived at. It is thus that the mathematicians proceed in reducing by analysis the theorems of speculation and the canons of practice into definitions, axioms, and postulates. Thus they come to simple ideas whose definition cannot be given; primitive truths that cannot be proved, and which do not need it, since they are identical propositions, whose opposite contains a manifest contradiction."

"But in contingent truths — those of fact — the sufficient reason must be found; namely, in the succession of things which fill the created universe, — for otherwise the analysis into particular reasons would go into detail without limit, by reason of the immense variety of natural things, and of the infinite divisibility of bodies. There are an infinity of figures and of past and present movements which enter into the efficient cause of my present writing, and there are an infinity of minute inclinations and dispositions of my soul which enter into its final cause. And since all this detail contains only other contingent and particular antecedents, each of which has need of a similar analysis to account for it, we really make no progress by this analysis; and it is necessary that the final or sufficient reason be outside the endless succession or series of contingent particulars, that it consist in a necessary being, in which this series of changes is contained only *eminenter*, as in its source. This necessary being and source is what we call God."

In other words, the tracing of empirical facts to their causes and conditions does not, after all, render them wholly rational. The series of causes is endless. Every condition is in turn conditioned. We are not so much solving the problem of the reason of a given fact, as we are stating the problem in other terms as we go on in this series. Every solution offers itself again as a problem, and this endlessly. If these truths of fact, then, are to be rendered wholly rational, it must be in something which lies outside of the series considered as a series; that is, something which is not an antecedent of any one of the series, but is equally related to each and to all as their ground and source. This, considered as an argument for the existence of God, we shall deal with hereafter; now we are concerned only with its bearing upon the relation of experience to the universality and necessity of knowledge. According to this, the ultimate meaning of facts is found in their relation to the divine intelligence; for Leibniz is emphatic in insisting that the relation of God to experience is not one of bare will to creatures produced by this will (as Descartes had supposed), but of a will governed wholly by Intelligence. As Leibniz states it in another connection, not only matters of fact, but mathematical truths, have the same final basis in the divine understanding.

"Such truths, strictly speaking, are only conditional, and say that in case their subject existed they would be found such and such. But if it is again asked in what consists this conditional connection in which there is necessary reality, the reply is that it is in the relation of ideas. And by the further question, Where would be the ideas if no spirit existed; and what would then become of the foundation of the certainty of such truths?—we are brought to the final foundation of truths; namely, that supreme and universal spirit, which must exist, and whose understanding is, in reality, the region of the eternal truths. And in order that it may not be thought that it is not necessary to have recourse to this region, we must consider that these necessary truths contain the determining reason and regulative principle of existence, and, in a word, of the laws of the universe. Thus these necessary truths, being anterior to the existences of contingent beings, must in turn be based upon the existence of a necessary substance."

It is because facts are not *mere* facts, in short, but are the manifestation of a "determining reason and regulative principle" which finds its home in universal intelligence, that knowledge of them can become necessary and general.

The general nature of truths of reason and of their ruling principle, identity and contradiction, has already been given in the quotation regarding the principle of sufficient reason. It is Leibniz's contention that only in truths whose opposite is seen to involve self-contradiction can we have absolute certainty, and that it is through connection with such eternal truths that the certainty of our other knowledge rests. It is thus evident why Leibniz insists, as against Locke, upon the great importance of axioms and maxims. They are important, not merely in themselves, but as the sole and indispensable bases of scientific truth regarding all matters. Leibniz at times, it is true, speaks as if demonstrative and contingent truths were of themselves, in principle, distinct, and even opposed. But he also corrects himself by showing that contingency is rather a subjective limitation than an objective quality. We, indeed, do not see that the truth "I exist," for example, is necessary, because we cannot see how its opposite involves contradiction. But "God sees how the two terms 'I' and 'exist' are connected; that is, *why* I exist." So far as we can see facts, then, from the standpoint of the divine intelligence, so far, it would appear, our knowledge is necessary.

Since these axioms, maxims, or first truths are "innate," we are in a condition to complete (for the first time) the discussion of innate ideas. These ideas constitute, as we have learned, the essential content of the divine intelligence, and of ours so far as we have realized our identity with God's understanding. The highest form of knowledge, therefore, is self-consciousness. This bears the same relation to necessary truths that the latter bear to experience. "Knowledge of necessary and eternal truths," says Leibniz, "distinguishes us from simple animals, and makes us have reason and science, *elevating us to the knowledge of ourselves.* We are thus developed to self-consciousness; and in being conscious of ourselves we are conscious of being, of substance, of the simple, of the spiritual, of God." And again he says that "those that know necessary truths are rational spirits, capable of self-consciousness, of recognizing what is termed Ego, substance, and monad. *Thus* they are rendered capable of demonstrative knowledge." "We are innate to ourselves; and since we are beings, being is innate to us, for knowledge of it is implicit in that which we have of ourselves."

Knowledge, in fine, may be regarded as an ascending series of four terms. The first is constituted by sensations associated together in such a way that a relation of antecedence and consequence exists between them. This is "experience." The second stage comes into existence when we connect these experiences, not by mere relations of "consecution," but by their conditions, by the principle of causality, and especially by that of sufficient reason, which connects them with the supreme intelligence, God. This stage is science. The third is knowledge of the axioms and necessary truths in and of themselves, not merely as involved in science. The fourth is self-consciousness, the knowledge of intelligence, in its intimate and universal nature, by which we know God, the mind, and all real substance. In the order of time the stage of experience is first, and that of self-consciousness last. But in the lowest stage there are involved the others. The progress of knowledge consists in the development or unfolding of this implicit content, till intelligence, spirit, activity, is clearly revealed as the source and condition of all.

CHAPTER XI.

THE THEOLOGY OF LEIBNIZ.

ONE of the chapters concerning knowledge is entitled, "The Knowledge that we have of God." This introduces us to the theology of Leibniz and indirectly to the completion of those ethical doctrines already outlined in the chapter on will. Leibniz employs three arguments to prove the existence of God: that of God as the sufficient reason of the world (substantially the cosmological proof); of God as the source of the pre-established harmony (an extension of the teleological proof); and the ontological. The latter he accepts as it came from the hands of Descartes, but insists that it requires an added argument before it ranks as anything more than presumptive proof. The Anselmic-Cartesian argument, as stated by Leibniz, is as follows: "God is defined as the greatest, or most perfect, of beings, or as a being of supreme grandeur and perfection. But in the notion of a perfect being, existence must be included, since it is something more to exist than not to exist. Or existence is a perfection, and hence must belong to the most perfect being; otherwise some perfection would be lacking, which is contrary to the definition." Or as Descartes sometimes puts it, in the notion of anything like a tree, a mountain, a triangle, contingency is contained. We may conceive such an object to exist or not, as we like. There is no necessity involved in our thought. But we cannot think of a perfect being except as existing. It does not rest with the decision of our thinking whether or not to include existence in this notion. We must necessarily think existence as soon as we think such a being.

Leibniz takes a middle position, he says, between those who consider this a demonstrative argument, and those who regard it as a mere paralogism. It is pre-supposed by this argument that the notion of a Supreme Being is possible, or that it does not involve contradiction. This pre-supposition is to be proved. First, it is well to simplify the argument itself. The Cartesian definition may be reduced to this: "God is a being in whom existence and essence are one. From this definition it follows as a corollary that such a being, if possible, exists. For the essence of a thing being just that which constitutes its possibility, it is evident that to exist by its essence is the same as to exist by its possibility. Being in itself, then, or God, may be most simply defined as the Being who must exist if he is possible."

There are two ways of proving this last clause (namely, that he is possible) the direct and the indirect. The indirect is employed against those who assert that from mere notions, ideas, definitions or possible essences, it is not possible to infer actual existence. Such persons simply deny the possibility of being in itself. But if being-in-itself, or absolute being, is impossible, being-by-another, or relative, is also impossible; for there is no "other" upon which it may depend. Nothing, in this case, could exist. Or if necessary being is not possible, there is no being possible. Put in another way, God is as necessary for possibility as for actual existence. If there is possibility of anything, there is God. This leads up to the direct proof; for it follows that, if there be a possibility of God, — the Being in whom existence and essence are one, — he exists. "God alone has such a position that existence is necessary, if possible. But since there can be nothing opposed to the possibility of a being without limit, — a being therefore without negations and without contradiction, — this is sufficient to prove *a priori* the existence of God." In short, God being pure affirmation, pure self-identity, the idea of his Being cannot include contradiction, and hence is possible, — and since possible, necessary. Of this conception of God as the purely self-identical, without negation, we shall have something to say in the next chapter.

The cosmological proof is, as we have already seen, that every cause in the world being at the same time an effect, it cannot be the sufficient reason of anything. The whole series is contingent, and requires a ground not prior to, but beyond, the series. The only *sufficient* reason of anything is that which is also the sufficient reason of itself,— absolute being. The teleological argument Leibniz invariably, I believe, presents in connection with the idea of pre-established harmony. "If the substances of experience," runs the argument, "had not received their being, both active and passive, from one universal supreme cause, they would be independent of one another, and hence would not exhibit that order, harmony, and beauty which we notice in nature. This argument possesses only moral certainty which becomes demonstrative by the new kind of harmony which I have introduced,—pre-established harmony. Since each substance expresses in its own way that which occurs beyond it, and can have no influence on other particular beings, it is necessary that each substance, before developing these phenomena from the depth of its own being, must have received this nature (this internal ground of external phenomena) from a universal cause from whom all beings depend, and which effects that one be perfectly in accord with and corresponding to every other. This cannot occur except through a being of infinite knowledge and power."

Having determined the existence of God, Leibniz states his attributes. These may be reduced to three. He is perfect in power, in wisdom, and in goodness. "Perfection is nothing other than the whole of positive reality separated from the limits and bounds of things. Where there are no limits, as in God, perfection is absolutely infinite." "In

God exists *power*, which is the source of all *knowledge*, — which comprehends the realm of ideas, down to its minutest detail, — and *will*, which directs all creations and changes according to the principle of the best." Or as he expands it at another time: "The supreme cause must be intelligent, for the existing world being contingent, and an infinity of other worlds being equally possible, it is necessary that the cause of the world take into consideration all these possible worlds in order to decide upon one. Now this relation of a substance to simple ideas must be the relation of understanding to its ideas, while deciding upon one is the act of will in choosing. Finally it is the power of this substance which executes the volition. Power has its end in being; wisdom, or understanding, in truth; and will in good. Thus the cause must be absolutely perfect in power, wisdom, and goodness. His understanding is the source of essences, and his will the origin of existences."

This brings us to the relation of God to the world, or to an account of the creating activity of God. This may be considered to be metaphysically, logically, or morally necessary. To say that it is metaphysically necessary is to say that it is the result of the divine essence, that it would imply a contradiction of the very being of God for the world not to be and not to be as it is. In short, the world becomes a mere emanation of power, since, as we have just learned, power and being are correlative. But this leaves out of account the divine understanding. Not all possible worlds emanate from God's being, but there is recognition of them and of their relations to one another. Were the world to proceed from the divine understanding alone, however, it would be logically necessary, — that is, it would bear the same relation to his understanding that necessary truths do. Its opposite would imply contradiction, not indeed of the being of God, but of his understanding. But the will of God plays the all-important part of choosing among the alternative worlds presented by reason, each of which is *logically* possible. One of these worlds, although standing on the same intellectual plane as the others, is *morally* better, — that is, it involves greater happiness and perfection to the creatures constituting it. God is guided then by the idea of the better (and this is the best possible) world. His will is not arbitrary in creating: it does not work by a *fiat* of brute power. But neither is it fatalistic: it does not work by compulsory necessity. It is both free and necessary; free, for it is guided by naught excepting God's own recognition of an end; necessary, for God, being God, cannot *morally* act otherwise than by the principle of the better, — and this in contingent matters is the best. Hence the optimism of Leibniz, to which here no further allusion can be made.

Since the best is precisely God himself, it is evident that the created world will have, *as far as possible*, his perfections. It would thus be possible to deduce from this conception of God and his relation to the world all those characteristics of the Leibnizian monadology which we formerly arrived at analytically. God is individual, but with an infinite comprehensiveness. Each substance repeats these properties of the supreme substance. There is an infinity of such substances, in order that the world may as perfectly as possible mirror the infinity of God. Each, so far as in it lies, reflects the activity of God; for activity is the very essence of perfection. And thus we might go through with the entire list of the properties of the monad.

To complete the present discussion, however, it is enough to notice that intelligence and will must be found in every creature, and that thus we account for the "appetition" and the "perception" that characterize even the lowest monad. The scale of monads, however, would not be as complete as possible unless there were beings in whom appetition became volition, and perception, self-conscious intelligence. Such monads will stand in quite other relation to God than the blind impulse-governed substances. "Spirits," says Leibniz, "are capable of entering into community with God, and God is related to them not only as an inventor to his machine (as he is to other creatures) but as a prince to his subjects, or, better, as a father to his children. This society of spirits constitutes the city of God, — the most perfect state under the most perfect monarch. This city of God, this truly cosmopolitan monarchy, is a moral world within the natural. Among all the works of God it is the most sublime and divine. In it consists the true glory of God, for there would be no glory of God unless his greatness and goodness were known and admired by spirits; and in his relation to this society, God for the first time reveals his goodness, while he manifests everywhere his power and wisdom. And as previously we demonstrated a perfect harmony between the two realms of nature, — those of efficient and final causes, — so must we here declare harmony between the physical realm of nature and the moral realm of grace, — that is, between God as the architect of the mechanical world-structure, and God as the monarch of the world of spirits." God fulfils his creation, in other words, in a realm of spirits, and fulfils it because here there are beings who do not merely reflect him but who enter into relations of companionship with him, forming a community. This community of spirits with one another and with God is the moral world, and we are thus brought again to the ethics of Leibniz.

It has been frequently pointed out that Leibniz was the first to give ethics the form which it has since kept in German philosophy, — the division into *Natur-recht* and *Natur-moral*. These terms are difficult to give in English, but the latter corresponds to what is ordinarily called "moral philosophy," while the former is political philosophy so far as that has an ethical bearing. Or the latter may be said to treat of the moral ideal and of the moral motive and of duty in themselves, while the former deals with the social, the public, and in a certain sense the external, aspects of morality.

Puffendorf undoubtedly suggested this division to Leibniz by his classification of duties as external and internal, — the first comprehending natural and civil law, the second moral theology. But Puffendorf confined the former to purely external acts, excluding motives and intentions, and the latter to divine revelation. Both are "positive," and in some sort arbitrary, — one resting merely on the fact that certain institutions obtain, the other on the fact that God has made certain declarations. To Leibniz, on the other hand, the will of God is in no sense the source of moral truths. The will of God does not create truth, but carries into effect the eternal truths of the divine understanding. Moral truths are like those of mathematics. And again, there is no such thing as purely external morality: it always contains an inner content, of which the external act is only the manifestation. Leibniz may thus be said to have made two discoveries, or rather re-discoveries: one, that there is a science of morals, independent of law, custom, and positive right; the other, that the basis of both "natural" and "positive" morals is not the mere will of God, but is reason with its content of eternal truths.

In morals the end is happiness, the means wisdom. Happiness is defined, not as an occurrence, but as a condition, or state of being. "It is the condition of permanent joy. This does not mean that the joy is actually felt every moment, but that one is in the condition to enjoy whenever he thinks of it, and that, in the interval, joyfulness arises from his activity and being." Pleasure, however, is not a state, but a feeling. It is the feeling of perfection, whether in ourselves or in anything else. It does not follow that we perceive intellectually either in what the perfection of the pleasant thing consists or in what way it develops perfection within us. It is enough that it be realized in feeling, so as to give us pleasure. Perfection is defined "as increase of being. As sickness is, as it were, a lowering and a falling off from health, so perfection is something which mounts above health. It manifests itself in power to act; for all substance consists in a certain power, and the greater the power the higher and freer the substance. But power increases in the degree that the many manifests itself from one and in one, while the one rules many from itself and transforms them into self. But unity in plurality is nothing else than harmony; and from this comes order or proportion, from which proceeds beauty, and beauty awakens love. Thus it becomes evident how happiness, pleasure, love, perfection, substance, power, freedom, harmony, proportion, and beauty are bound up in one another."

From this condensed sketch, taken from Leibniz himself, the main features of his ethical doctrine clearly appear. When we were studying freedom we saw that it was not so much a starting-point of the will as its goal and ideal. We saw also that true freedom is dependent upon knowledge, upon recognition of the eternal and universal. What we have here is a statement of that doctrine in terms of feeling and of will instead of knowledge. The end of man is stated to be happiness, but the notion of happiness is developed in such a way that it is seen to be equivalent to the Aristotelian notion of self-realization; "it is development of substance, and substance is activity." It is the union of one and the many; and the one, according to the invariable doctrine of Leibniz, is the spiritual element, and the many is the real content which gives meaning to this rational unity. Happiness thus means perfection, and perfection a completely universalized individual. The motive toward the moral life is elsewhere stated to be love; and love is defined as interest in perfection, and hence culminates in love of God, the only absolute perfection. It also has its source in God, as the origin of perfection; so that Leibniz says, Whoso loves God, loves all.

Natural right, as distinguished from morals, is based upon the notion of justice, this being the outward manifestation of wisdom, or knowledge, — appreciation of the relation of actions to happiness. The definitions given by Leibniz are as follows: Just and unjust are what are useful or harmful to the public, — that is, to the community of spirits. This community includes first God, then humanity, then the state. These are so subordinated that, in cases of collision of duty, God, the universe of relations, comes before the profit of humanity, and this before the state. At another time Leibniz defines justice as social virtue, and says that there are as many kinds of "right" as there are kinds of natural communities in which happiness is an end of action. A natural community is defined as one which rests upon desire and the power of satisfying it, and includes three varieties, — domestic, civil, and ecclesiastic. "Right" is defined as that which sustains and develops any natural community. It is, in other words, the will for happiness united with insight into what makes happiness.

Corresponding to the three forms of the social organism (as we should now call the "natural community"), are the three kinds of *jus*, — *jus strictum*, equity, and piety. Each of these has its corresponding prescript. That of *jus strictum* is to injure no one; of equity, to render to each his own; and of piety, to make the ethical law the law of conduct. *Jus strictum* includes the right of war and peace. The right of peace exists between individuals till one breaks it. The right of war exists between men and things. The victory of person over thing is *property*. Things thus come to possess the right of the person to whom they belong as against every other person; that is, in the right of the person to himself as against the attacks of another (the right to peace) is included a right to his property. *Jus strictum* is, of course, in all cases, enforceable by civil law and the compulsory force which accompanies it. Equity, however, reaches beyond this to obligation in cases where there is no right of compulsion. Its law is, Be of aid to all, but to each according to his merits and his claims. Finally comes piety. The other two stages are limited. The lowest is negative, it wards off harm; the second aims after happiness, but only within the limits of earthly existence. That we should ourselves bear misery, even the greatest, for the sake of others, and should subject the whole of this existence to something higher, cannot be proved excepting as we regard the society, or community, of our spirits with God. Justice with relation to God comprehends all virtues. Everything that is, is from God; and hence the law of all conduct is to use everything according to its place in the idea of God, according to its function in the universal harmony. It thus not only complements the other two kinds of justice but is the source of their inner ethical worth. "Strict justice" may conflict with equity. But God effects that what is of use to the public well-being — that is, to the universe and to humanity — shall be of use also to the individual. Thus from the standpoint of God the moral is advantageous, and the immoral hurtful. Kant's indebtedness to Leibniz will at once appear to one initiated into the philosophy of the former.

Leibniz never worked out either his ethics or his political philosophy in detail; but it is evident that they both take their origin and find their scope in the fact of man's relationship to God, that they are both, in fact, accounts of the methods of realizing a universal but not a merely formal harmony. For harmony is not, with Leibniz, an external arrangement, but is the very soul of being. Perfect harmony, or adaptation to the universe of relations, is the end of the individual, and man is informed of his progress toward this end by an inner sentiment of pleasure.

It may be added that Leibniz's æsthetic theory, so far as developed, rests upon the same basis as his ethical,—namely, upon membership in the "city of God," or community of spiritual beings. This is implied, indeed, in a passage already quoted, where he states the close connection of beauty with harmony and perfection. The feeling of beauty is the recognition in feeling of an order, proportion, and harmony which are not yet intellectually descried. Leibniz illustrates by music, the dance, and architecture. This feeling of the harmonious also becomes an impulse to produce. As perception of beauty may be regarded as unexplained, or confused, perception of truth, so creation of beauty may be considered as undeveloped will. It is action on its way to perfect freedom, for freedom is simply activity with explicit recognition of harmony.

We cannot do better than quote the conclusion of the matter from Leibniz's "Principles of Nature and of Grace," although, in part, it repeats what we have already learned. "There is something more in the rational soul, or spirit, than there is in the monad or even in the simple soul. Spirit is not only a mirror of the universe of creatures, but is also an image of the divine being. Spirit not only has a perception of the works of God, but is also capable of producing something which resembles them, though on a small scale. To say nothing of dreams, in which we invent without trouble and without volition things upon which we must reflect a long time in order to discover in our waking state,— to say nothing of this, our soul is architectonic in voluntary actions; and, in discovering the sciences in accordance with which God has regulated all things (*pondere*, *mensura*, *numero*), it imitates in its department and in its own world of activity that which God does in the macrocosm. This is the reason why spirits, entering through reason and eternal truths into a kind of society with God, are members of the city of God,—that is, of the most perfect state, formed and governed by the best of monarchs, in which there is no crime without punishment, and no good action without reward, and where there is as much of virtue and of happiness as may possibly exist. And this occurs not through a disturbance of nature, as if God's dealing with souls were in violation of mechanical laws, but by the very order of natural things, on account of the eternal, pre-established harmony between the kingdoms of nature and grace, between God as monarch and God as architect, since nature leads up to grace, and grace makes nature perfect in making use of it."

No better sentences could be found with which to conclude this analysis of Leibniz. They resound not only with the grandeur and wide scope characteristic of his thought, but they contain his essential idea, his pre-eminent "note," — that of the harmony of the natural and the supernatural, the mechanical and the organic. The mechanical is to Leibniz what the word signifies; it is the *instrumental*, and this in the full meaning of the term. Nature is instrumental in that it performs a function, realizes a purpose, and instrumental in the sense that without it spirit, the organic, is an empty dream. The spiritual, on the other hand, is the meaning, the *idea* of nature. It perfects it, in that it makes it instrumental to itself, and thus renders it not the passive panorama of *mere* material force, but the manifestation of living spirit.

CHAPTER XII.

CRITICISM AND CONCLUSION.

IN the exposition now completed we have in general taken for granted the truth and coherency of Leibniz's fundamental ideas, and have contented ourselves with an account of the principles and notions that flow from these ideas. The time has come for retracing our steps, and for inquiring whether the assumed premises can be thus unquestioningly adopted. This final chapter, therefore, we shall devote to criticism of the basis of Leibniz's philosophy, not attempting to test it by a comparison with other systems, but by inquiring into its internal coherency, and by a brief account of the ways in which his successors, or at least one of them, endeavored to make right the points in which he appeared to fail.

The fundamental contradiction in Leibniz is to be found, I believe, between the method which he adopted — without inquiry into its validity and scope — and the subject-matter, or perhaps better the attitude, to which he attempted to apply this method; between, that is to say, the scholastic formal logic on the one hand and the idea of inter-relation derived from the development of scientific thought, on the other. Leibniz never thought of investigating the formal logic bequeathed by scholasticism, with a view to determining its adequacy as philosophic method. He adopted, as we have seen, the principles of identity and contradiction as sole principles of the only perfect knowledge. The type of knowledge is that which can be reduced to a series of identical propositions, whose opposite is seen to be impossible, because self-contradictory. Only knowledge in this form can be said to be demonstrative and necessary. As against Locke he justified the syllogistic method of the schoolmen as the typical method of all rational truth.

On the other hand, Leibniz, as we saw in the earlier chapters, had learned positively from the growth of science, negatively from the failures of Descartes and Spinoza, to look upon the universe as a unity of inter-related members, — as an organic unity, not a mere self-identical oneness. Failing to see the cause of the failures of Descartes and Spinoza in precisely their adoption of the logic of identity and contradiction as ultimate, he attempted to reconcile this method with the conception of organic activity. The result is constant conflict between the method and content of his philosophy, between its letter and its spirit. The contradiction is a twofold one. The unity of the content of his philosophy, the conception of organism or harmony, is a unity which essentially involves difference. The unity of his method is a formal identity which excludes it. The unity, whose discovery constitutes

Leibniz's great glory as a philosopher, is a unity of activity, a dynamic process. The unity of formal logic is exclusive of any mediation or process, and is essentially rigid and lifeless. The result is that Leibniz is constantly wavering (in logical result, not of course in spirit) between two opposed errors, one of which is, in reality, not different from Spinozism, in that it regards all distinction as only phenomenal and unreal, while the other is akin to atomism, in that attempting to avoid the doctrine of the all-inclusive one, it does so only by supposing a multitude of unrelated units, termed monads. And thus the harmony, which in Leibniz's intention is the very content of reality, comes to be, in effect, an external arrangement between the one and the many, the unity and the distinction, in themselves incapable of real relations. Such were the results of Leibniz's failure, in Kantian language, to criticise his categories, in Hegelian language, to develop a logic, — the results of his assuming, without examination, the validity of formal logic as a method of truth.

So thoroughly is Leibniz imbued with the belief in its validity, that the very conception, that of sufficient reason, which should have been the means of saving him from his contradictions, is used in such a way as to plunge him deeper into them. The principle of sufficient reason may indeed be used as purely formal and external, — as equivalent to the notion that everything, no matter what, has *some* explanation. Thus employed, it simply declares that everything has *a* reason, without in the least determining the *what* of that reason, — its content. This is what we mean by calling it formal. But this is not the way in which Leibniz conceives of it. According to him, it is not a principle of the external connection of one finite, or phenomenal, fact with another. It is a principle in the light of which the whole phenomenal world is to be viewed, declaring that its ground and meaning are to be found in reason, in self-conscious intelligence. As we have seen, it is equivalent, in Leibniz's case, to the notion that we have no complete nor necessary knowledge of the world of scientific fact until we have referred it to a conditioning "Supreme Spirit."

Looked at in this way, we see that the unity which Leibniz is positively employing is an organic unity, a unity of intelligence involving organic reference to the known world. But such a conception of sufficient reason leaves no place for the final validity of identity and non-contradiction; and therefore Leibniz, when dealing with his method, and not, as in the passages referred to, with his subject-matter, cannot leave the matter thus. To do so indeed would have involved a complete reconstruction of his philosophy, necessitating a derivation of all the categories employed from intelligence itself (that is, from the sufficient or conditioning reason). But the bondage to scholastic method is so great that Leibniz can see no way but to measure intelligence by the ready-made principle of identity, and thus virtually (though not in purpose) to explain away the very principle of sufficient reason. In Leibniz's words: "Contingent truths require an infinite analysis which only God can carry out. Whence by him alone are they known *a priori* and demonstratively. For although the reason can always be found for some occurring state in a prior state, this reason again requires a reason, and we never arrive in the series to the ultimate reason. But this *progressus ad infinitum* takes (in us) the place of a sufficient reason, which can be found only outside the series in God, on whom all its members, prior and posterior depend, rather than upon one another. *Whatever truth, therefore, is incapable of analysis, and cannot be demonstrated from its own reasons, but has its ultimate reason and certainty only from the divine mind, is not necessary.* Everything that we call truths of fact come under this head, and this is the root of their contingency."

The sentences before the one italicized repeat what we have learned before, and seem to convey the idea that the phenomenal world is that which does not account for itself, because not itself a self-determining reason, and which gets its ultimate explanation and ground in a self-sufficient reason, — God. But notice the turn given to the thought with the word "therefore." Therefore all truth incapable of analysis, — that is, of reduction to identical propositions, whose opposite is impossible because self-contradictory, — all truth whose meaning depends upon not its bare identity, but upon its relation to the very content of all intelligence, is not necessary, but contingent. Leibniz here distinctly opposes identical truths as necessary, to truth connected with reason as contingent. Synthetic reference to the very structure of intelligence is thus made, not the ground of truth, but a blot upon its completeness and necessity. Perfect truth, it is implied in the argument, is self-identical, known by mere analysis of itself, and needs no reference to an organism of reason. The reference, therefore, to a principle of sufficient reason is simply a concession to the fragmentary and imperfect condition of all knowledge. Truth in itself is self-identical; but appearing to us only confusedly, we employ the idea of sufficient reason as a makeshift, by which we refer, in a mass, all that we cannot thus reduce to identical propositions, to an intelligence, or to a *Deus ex machina* which can so reduce it. This is the lame and impotent conclusion.

Leibniz's fundamental meaning is, no doubt, a correct one. He means that contingency of fact is not real, but apparent; that it exists only because of our inability to penetrate the reason which would enable us completely to account for the facts under consideration. He *means* that if we could understand, *sub specie aeternitatis*, from the standpoint of universal intelligence, we should see every fact as necessary, as resulting from an intrinsic reason. But so thoroughly is he fettered by the scholastic method — that is, the method of formal logic — that he can conceive of this immanent and intrinsic reason which makes every fact a truth — that is, self-evident in its necessity — only as an analytic, self-contained identity. And herein lies his contradiction: his method obliges him to conceive of ultimate intelligence as purely formal, simply as that which does not contradict itself, while the attitude of his thought and its concrete subject-matter compel him to think of intelligence as possessing a content, as the organic unity of a system of relations.

From this contradiction flow the other contradictions of Leibniz, which we are now prepared to examine in more detail. For his ideas are so much greater than his method that in almost every point there seems to be contradiction. His ideas *per se* mean one thing, and his ideas as interpreted by his method another. Take his doctrine of individuality, for instance. To some it has appeared that the great defect of the Leibnizian philosophy is its individualism. Such conceive him simply to have carried out in his monadism the doctrine of the individual isolated from the universe to its logical conclusions, and thereby to have rendered it absurd. In a certain sense, the charge is true. The monad, according to the oft-repeated statement, has no intercourse with the rest of the universe. It really excludes all else. It acts as if nothing but itself and God were in existence. That is to say, the monad, being the self-identical, must shut out all intrinsic or real relations with other substances. Such relations would involve a differentiating principle for which Leibniz's logic has no place. Each monad is, therefore, an isolated universe. But such a result has no value for Leibniz. He endeavors to correct it by the thought that each monad *ideally* includes the whole universe by mirroring it. And then to reconcile the real exclusion and the ideal inclusion, he falls back on a *Deus ex machina* who arranges a harmony between them, foreign to the intrinsic nature of each. Leibniz's individualism, it is claimed, thus makes of his philosophy a synthesis, or rather a juxtaposition, of mutually contradictory positions, each of which appears true only as long as we do not attempt to think it together with the other.

There is, no doubt, truth in this representation. But a more significant way of stating the matter is, I think, that Leibniz's defect is not in his individualism, but in the defect of his conception of the individual. His individualism is more apparent than real. It is a negative principle, and negative in the sense of *privative*. The individuality of the monad is due to its incompleteness, to its imperfections. It is really matter which makes monads mutually impenetrable or exclusive; it is matter which distinguishes them from God, and thus from one another. Without the material element they would be lost in an undistinguished identity with God, the supreme substance. But matter, it must be remembered, is passivity; and since activity is reality, or substance, matter is unsubstantial and unreal. The same results from a consideration of knowledge. Matter is always correlative to confused ideas. With the clearing up of knowledge, with making it rational, matter must disappear, so that to God, who is wholly reason, it must entirely vanish. But this view varies only in words from that of Spinoza, to whom it is the imagination, as distinguished from the intellect, that is the source of particular and finite objects.

It is perhaps in his *Theodicée*, in the treatment of the problem of evil, that his implicit Spinozism, or denial of individuality, comes out most clearly. That evil is negative, or privative, and consists in the finitude of the creature, is the result of the discussion. What is this except to assert the unreality, the merely privative character, of the finite, and to resolve all into God? To take one instance out of many: he compares inertia to the original limitation of creatures, and says that as inertia is the obstacle to the complete mobility of bodies, so privation, or lack, constitutes the essence of the imperfection, or evil, of creatures. His metaphor is of boats in the current of a river, where the heavier one goes more slowly, owing to inertia. The force of the current, which is the same to all, and which is positive, suffering no diminution, is comparable to the activity of God, which also is perfect and positive. As the current is the positive source of all the movements of the bodies, and is in no way responsible for the retardation of some boats, so God is the source only of activities, — the perfections of his creatures. "As the inertia of the boat is the cause of its slowness, so the limitations of its receptivity are the cause of the defects found in the action of creatures." Individuality is thus reduced to mere limitation; and the unlimited, the real which includes all reality, is God. We are thus placed in a double difficulty. This notion of an all-inclusive one contradicts the reality of mutually exclusive monads; and we have besides the characteristic difficulty of Spinoza,—how, on the basis of this unlimited, self-identical substance, to account for even the appearance of finitude, plurality and individuality.

Leibniz's fundamental defect may thus be said to be that, while he realized, as no one before him had done, the importance of the conception of the *negative*, he was yet unable to grasp the significance of the negative, was led to interpret it as merely privative or defective, and thus, finally, to surrender the very idea. Had not his method, his presupposition regarding analytic identity, bound him so completely in its toils, his clear perception that it was the negative element that differentiated God from the universe, intelligence from matter, might have brought him to a general anticipation not only of Kant, but of Hegel. But instead of transforming his method by this conception of negation, he allowed his assumed (*i. e.*, dogmatic) method to evacuate his conception of its significance. It was Hegel who was really sufficiently in earnest with the idea to read it into the very notion of intelligence as a constituent organic element, not as a mere outward and formal limitation.

We have already referred to the saying of Leibniz that the monad acts as if nothing existed but God and itself. The same idea is sometimes expressed by saying that God alone is the immediate or direct object of the monad. Both expressions mean that, while the monad excludes all other monads, such is not the case in its relation to God, but that it has an organic relation with him. We cannot keep from asking whether there is not another aspect of the contradiction here. How is it possible for the monad so to escape from its isolation that it can have communication with God more than with other substances? Or if it can have communication with God, why cannot it equally bear real relations of community with other monads? And the answer is found in Leibniz's contradictory conceptions of God. Of these conceptions there are at least three. When Leibniz is emphasizing his monadic theory, with its aspects of individuality and exclusion, God is conceived as the highest monad, as one in the series of monads, differing from the others only in the degree of its activity. He is the "monad of monads"; the most complete, active, and individualized of all. But it is evident that in this sense there can be no more intercourse between God and a monad than there is between one monad and another. Indeed, since God is *purus actus* without any passivity, it may be said that there is, if possible, less communication in this case than in the others. He is, as Leibniz says, what a monad without matter would be, "a deserter from the general order." He is the acme of isolation. This, of course, is the extreme development of the "individual" side of Leibniz's doctrine, resulting in a most pronounced atomism. Leibniz seems dimly conscious of this difficulty, and thus by the side of this notion of God he puts another. According to it, God is the source of all monads. The monads are not created by a choice of the best of all possible worlds, as his official theology teaches, but are the radiations of his divinity. Writing to Bayle, Leibniz expresses himself as follows: "The nature of substance consists in an active force of definite character, from which phenomena proceed in orderly succession. This force was originally received by, and is indeed preserved to, every substance by the creator of all things, from whom all *actual forces or perfections emanate by a sort of continual creation.*" And in his Monadology he says: All "the created or derived monads are the productions of God, and are born, as it were, *by the continual fulgurations of the divinity from instant to instant*, bounded by the receptivity of the creature to which it is essential to be limited." What has become of the doctrine of monads (although the word is retained) it would be difficult to say. There is certainly no individual distinction now between the created monads and God, and it is impossible to see why there should be individual distinctions between the various created monads. They appear to be all alike, as modes of the one comprehensive substance. Here we have the universal, or "identity," side of

Leibniz's philosophy pushed to its logical outcome, — the doctrine of pantheism.

His third doctrine of God is really a unity of the two previous. It is the doctrine that God is the harmony of the monads, — neither one among them nor one made up of them, but their organic unity. This doctrine is nowhere expressly stated in words (unless it be when he says that "God alone constitutes the relation and community of substances"), but it runs through his whole system. According to this, God *is* the pre-established harmony. This conception, like that of harmony, may have either a mechanical interpretation (according to which God is the artificial, external point of contact of intelligence and reality, in themselves opposed) or an organic meaning, according to which God *is* the unity of intelligence and reality. On this interpretation alone does the saying that God is the only immediate object of the monads have sense. It simply states that the apparent dualism between intelligence and its object which is found in the world is overcome in God; that the distinction between them is not the ultimate fact, but exists in and for the sake of a unity which transcends the difference. According to this view, the opposition between ideal inclusion and real exclusion vanishes. God *is* the harmony of the real and ideal, not a mere arrangement for bringing them to an understanding with one another. Individuality and universality are no longer opposed conceptions, needing a *tertium quid* to relate them, but are organic factors of reality, and this, at the same time, is intelligence.

But admitting this conception as stating the implicit intention of Leibniz, the relation of monads to one another is wholly different from that which Leibniz gives. And to this point we now come. If in God, the absolute, the real and the ideal are one, it is impossible that in substances, which have their being and significance only in relation to God, or this unity, the real and the ideal should be so wholly separated as Leibniz conceives.

Leibniz's conception relative to this is, as we have seen, that there is no physical *influxus*, or *commercium*, of monads, but ideal consensus. *Really* each shuts out every other; *ideally*, or representatively, it includes every other. His positive thought in the matter is that a complete knowledge of any portion of the universe would involve a perfect knowledge of the whole, so organic is the structure of the universe. Each monad sums up the past history of the world, and is big with its future. This is the conception of inter-relation; the conception of all in one, and one as a member, not a part of a whole. It is the conception which Leibniz brought to birth, the conception of the thorough unity of the world. In this notion there is no denial of community of relation; it is rather the culmination of relation. There is no isolation. But according to his presupposed logic, individuality can mean only identity excluding distinction,—identity without intrinsic relation, and, as Leibniz is bound at all hazards to save the notion of individuality, he is obliged to think of this inter-relation as only ideal, as the result of a predetermined tendency given at its creation to the self-identical monad by God. But of course Leibniz does not escape the contradiction between identity and distinction, between individuality and universality, by this means. He only transfers it to another realm. In the relation of the monad to God the diversity of its content, the real or universal element, is harmonized with the identity of its law, its ideal or individual factor. But if these elements do not conflict here, why should they in the relation of the monads to one another? Either there is already an immanent harmony between the individual and universal, and no external arrangement is needed to bring it about, or there is no such harmony, and therefore no relation possible between God and the individual monad. One side of the Leibnizian philosophy renders the other side impossible.

Another consequence of Leibniz's treatment of the negative as merely limitative is that he can find no distinction, excepting of degree, between nature and spirit. Such a conception is undoubtedly in advance of the Cartesian dualism, which regards them as opposed realms *without* any relation; but it may be questioned whether it is as adequate a view as that which regards them as distinct realms *on account* of relation. At all events, it leads to confusion in Leibniz's treatment of both material objects and self-conscious personalities. In the former case his method of escape is a metaphor, — that objects apparently material are full of souls, or spirits. This may mean that the material is *merely* material only when considered in implicit abstraction from the intelligence which conditions it, that the material, in truth, is constituted by some of the relations which in their completeness make up intelligence. This at least bears a consistent meaning. But it is not monadism; it is not the doctrine that matter differs from spirit only in degree: it is the doctrine that they differ in kind, as the conditioned from the conditioning. At times, however, Leibniz attempts to carry out his monadism literally, and the result is that he conceives matter as being itself endowed, in some unexplained way, with souls, or since this implies a dualism between matter and soul, of being made up, composed, of souls. But as he is obliged to explain that this composition is not spatial, or physical, but only ideal, this doctrine tends to resolve itself into the former. And thus we end where we began, — with a metaphor.

On the other hand there is a wavering treatment of the nature of spirit. At times it is treated as precisely on a level in kind with the monads that "compose" matter, differing only in the greater degree of its activity. But at other times it is certainly represented as standing on another plane. "The difference between those monads which express the world with consciousness and those which express it unintelligently is as great as the difference between a mirror and one who sees." If Leibniz means what he seems to imply by these words, it is plainly asserted that only the spiritual being is worthy of being called a monad, or individual, at all, and that material being is simply a dependent manifestation of spirit. Again he says: "Not all entelechies are, like our soul, *images of God*, — being made as members of a society or state of which he is chief, — but all are *images of the universe*." In this distinction between self-conscious beings as images of God and unconscious monads as images of the universe there is again implied a difference of kind. That something is the image of the universe need mean only that it cannot be explained without its relations to the universe. To say that something is the image of God, must mean that it is itself spiritual and self-conscious. God alone is reason and activity. He alone has his reality in himself. Self-conscious beings, since members of a community with him, must participate in this reality in a way different in kind from those things which, at most, are only substances or objects, not subjects.

Nor do the difficulties cease here. If matter be conceived, not as implied in the relations by which reason is realized in constituting the universe, but as itself differing from reason only in degree, it is impossible to account for its existence. Why should a less degree of perfection exist than is necessary? Why should not the perfect activity, God, complete the universe in himself? Leibniz's answer that an infinity of monads multiplies his existence so far as possible, may hold indeed of other spirits, who mirror him and live in one divine society, but is utterly inapplicable to those which fail to image him. Their existence, as material, is merely privative; it is merely the absence of the activity found in conscious spirit. How can this deprivation, this limitation, increase in any way the harmony and perfection of the universe? Leibniz's theory of the negative, in fine, compels him to put nature and spirit on the same level, as differing only in degree. This, so far from giving nature a reality, results in its being swallowed up in spirit, not as necessarily distinct from it and yet one with it, but as absorbed in it, since the apparent difference is only privative. Nor does the theory insure the reality of spirit. This, since one in kind with matter, is swallowed up along with it in the one substance, which is positive and self-identical, — in effect, the *Deus sive Natura* of Spinoza.

We have to see that this contradiction on the side of existence has its correlate on the side of knowledge, and our examination of this fundamental deficiency in Leibniz is ended. Sensation is on the side of intelligence what matter is on the side of reality. It is confused knowledge, as matter is imperfect activity or reality. Knowledge is perfect only when it is seen to be necessary, and by "necessary" is meant that whose opposite is impossible, or involves contradiction. In spite, therefore, of Leibniz's thorough conviction that "matters of fact" — the subject-matter of physical science — are not arbitrary, he is yet obliged finally to agree with Locke that there is no certainty to be found in such knowledge, either as a whole or in any of its details. The element of sensation, of confused knowledge, cannot be eliminated. Hence it must always be open to any one to object that it is only on account of this imperfect factor of our knowledge that there appears to be a physical world at all, that the external world is an illusion produced by our sensations. And Leibniz himself, while claiming that the world of fact, as opposed to the realm of relations, possesses *practical* reality, is obliged to admit that *metaphysically* it may be only an orderly dream. The fact is that Leibniz unconsciously moves in the same circle, with relation to sensation and the material world, that confines Spinoza with regard to imagination and particular multiple existences. Spinoza explains the latter from that imperfection of our intelligence which leads us to imagine rather than to think. But he accounts for the existence of imagination, when he comes to treat that, as due to the plurality of particular things. So Leibniz, when an account of the existence of matter is demanded of him, refers to confused knowledge as its source, while in turn he explains the latter, or sensation, from the material element which sets bounds to the activity of spirit. Leibniz seems indeed, to advance upon Spinoza in admitting the reality of the negative factor in differentiating the purely self-identical, but he gives up what he has thus gained by interpreting the negation as passivity, or mere deprivation.

To sum up, it may be doubted whether we have more to learn from Leibniz's successes or from his failures. Leibniz's positive significance for us is in his clear recognition of the problems of modern philosophy, and in his perception of the isolated elements of their solution. His negative significance is in his clinging to a method which allowed him only to juxtapose these elements without forming of them a true synthesis. There are a number of sides from which we may state Leibniz's realization of the problem. Perhaps that which distinguishes Leibniz most clearly from Locke is their respective treatments of the relation of the physical to the spiritual, or, as the question presented itself mainly to them, of the "natural" to the "supernatural." To Locke the supernatural was strictly miraculous; it was, from our standpoint, mere power, or will. It might indeed be rational, but this reason was incapable of being apprehended by us. Its distinction from the finite was so great that it could be conceived only as something preceding and succeeding the finite in time, and meanwhile as intercalating itself arbitrarily here and there into the finite; as, for example, in the relation of soul and body, in the production of sensation, etc. In a word, Locke thought that the ends of philosophy, and with it of religion and morals, could be attained only by a complete separation of the "natural" and the "supernatural." Leibniz, on the other hand, conceived the aim of philosophy to be the demonstration of their harmony. This is evidenced by his treatment of the relations of the infinite and finite, of matter and spirit, of mechanical and final causation. And he found the sought-for harmony in the fact that the spiritual is the reason, purpose, and function of the natural. The oft-quoted words of Lotze express the thought of Leibniz: "The mechanical is unbounded in range, but is subordinate in value." We cannot find some things that occur physically, and others that occur supernaturally; everything that occurs has its sufficient mechanical antecedents, but all that occurs has its significance, its purpose, in something that does not occur, but that eternally is — Reason. The mechanical and the spiritual are not realms which here and there come into outward contact. They are related as the conditioned and the conditioning. That, and not the idea of an artificial *modus vivendi*, is the true meaning of the pre-established harmony.

In other words, Leibniz's great significance for us is the fact that, although he accepted in good faith, and indeed as himself a master in its methods, the results and principles of physical science, he remained a teleological idealist of the type of Aristotle. But I have not used the right words. It was not in spite of his acceptance of the scientific view of the world that he retained his faith in the primacy of purpose and reason. On the contrary, he was an idealist because of his science, because only by the idea of an all-conditioning spiritual activity could he account for and make valid scientific conceptions; he was a teleologist, because natural processes, with their summing up in the notion of causality, were meaningless except as manifesting an immanent purpose.

There are other more technical ways of stating the bearing of Leibniz's work. We may say that he realized that the problem of philosophy consisted in giving due value to the notions of individuality and universality, of identity and difference, or of the real and the ideal. In developing these ideas, however, we should only be repeating what has already been said, and so we may leave the matter here. On the negative side we need only recall what was said a few pages back regarding the incompatibility of Leibniz's method — the scholastic formal logic — with the content of his philosophy. The attempt to find a formal criterion of truth was hopeless; it was worse than fruitless, for it led to such an interpretation of concrete truths as to deprive them of their significance and as to land Leibniz in involved contradictions.

To write a complete account of the influence of Leibniz's philosophy would be too large a task for these pages. If we were to include under this head all the ramifications of thought to which Leibniz stimulated, directly and indirectly, either by stating truths which some one worked out or by stating errors which incited some one to new points of view, we should have to sketch German philosophy since his time, — and not only the professional philosophy, but those wide aspects of thought which were reflected in Herder, Lessing, and Goethe. It is enough to consider him as the forerunner of Kant. It has become so customary to represent Kant as working wholly on the problem which Hume presented, that his great indebtedness to Leibniz is overlooked. Because Hume aroused Kant from his dogmatic slumbers, it is supposed that Kant threw off the entire influence of the Leibnizian thought as vain dreams of his sleep. Such a representation is one-sided. It is truer to state that Hume challenged Kant to discover the method by which he could justify the results of Leibniz. In this process, the results, no doubt, took on a new form: results are always relative to method; but Kant never lost sight of the results. In the main, he accepted the larger features of the Leibnizian conclusions, and, taught by Hume of the insufficiency of the method that Leibniz followed, searched for a method which should guarantee them.

This aspect of Kant appears more fully in his lesser and somewhat controversial writings than in his classic works; and this, no doubt, is one reason that his indebtedness is so often overlooked. His close relation to Leibniz appears most definitely in his *brochure* entitled "Concerning a Discovery which renders Unnecessary all Critique of Pure Reason." A Wolffian, Eberhard by name, had "made the discovery" (to use Kant's words) "that the Leibnizian philosophy contained a critique of reason just as well as the modern, and accordingly contained everything that is true in the latter, and much else in addition." In his reply to this writing, Kant takes the position that those who claimed to be Leibnizians simply repeated the words of Leibniz without penetrating into his spirit, and that consequently they misrepresented him on every important point. He, Kant, on the other hand, making no claim to use the terminology of Leibniz, was his true continuator, since he had only changed the doctrine of the latter so as to make it conform to the true intent of Leibniz, by removing its self-contradictions. He closes: "'The Critique of Pure Reason' may be regarded as the real apology for Leibniz, even against his own professed followers."

Kant, in particular, names three points in which he is the true follower of Leibniz. The professed disciples of the latter insisted that the law of sufficient reason was an objective law, a law of nature. But, says Kant, it is so notorious, so self-evident, that no one can make a new discovery through this principle, that Leibniz can have meant it only as subjective. "For what does it mean to say that over and above the principle of contradiction another principle must be employed? It means this: that, according to the principle of contradiction, only that can be known which is already contained in the notion of the object; if anything more is to be known, it must be sought through the use of a special principle, distinct from that of contradiction. Since this last kind of knowledge is that of synthetic principles, Leibniz means just this: besides the principle of contradiction, or that of analytic judgments, there must be another, that of sufficient reason, for synthetic judgments. He thus pointed out, in a new and remarkable manner, that certain investigations in metaphysics were still to be made." In other words, Kant, by his distinction of analytic and synthetic judgments, with their respective principles and spheres, carried out the idea of Leibniz regarding the principles of contradiction and sufficient reason.

The second point concerns the relation of monads to material bodies. Eberhard, like the other professed Leibnizians, interpreted Leibniz as saying that corporeal bodies, as composite, are actually made up out of monads, as simple. Kant, on the other hand, saw clearly that Leibniz was not thinking of a relation of composition, but of condition. "He did not mean the material world, but the substrate, the intellectual world which lies in the idea of reason, and in which everything must be thought as consisting of simple substances." Eberhard's process, he says, is to begin with sense-phenomena, to find a simple element as a part of the sense-perceptions, and then to present this simple element as if it were spiritual and equivalent to the monad of Leibniz. Kant claims to follow the thought of Leibniz in regarding the simple not as an element *in* the sensuous, but as something super-sensuous, the *ground* of the sensuous. Leibniz's mistake was that, not having worked out clearly the respective limits of the principles of identity and of sufficient reason, he supposed that we had a direct intellectual intuition of this super-sensuous, when in reality it is unknowable.

The third group of statements concerns the principle of pre-established harmony. "Is it possible," asks Kant, "that Leibniz meant by this doctrine to assert the mere coincidence of two substances wholly independent of each other by nature, and incapable through their own force of being brought into community?" And his answer is that what Leibniz really implied was not a harmony between independent things, but a harmony between modes of knowing, between sense on the one hand and understanding on the other. The "Critique of Pure Reason" carried the discussion farther by pointing out its grounds; namely, that, without the unity of sense and understanding, no experience would be possible. *Why* there should be this harmony, *why* we should have experience, this question it is impossible to answer, says Kant, — adding that Leibniz confessed as much when he called it a "pre-established" harmony, thus not explaining it, but only referring it to a highest cause. That Leibniz really means a harmony within intelligence, not a harmony of things by themselves, is made more clear, according to Kant, from the fact that it is applied also to the relation between the kingdom of nature and of grace, of final and of efficient causes. Here the harmony is clearly not between two independently existing *external things*, but between what flows from our notions of nature (*Naturbegriffe*) and of freedom (*Freiheitsbegriffe*); that is, between two distinct powers and principles *within us*, — an agreement which can be explained only through the idea of an intelligent cause of the world.

If we review these points in succession, the influence of Leibniz upon Kant becomes more marked. As to the first one, it is well known that Kant's philosophy is based upon, and revolves within, the distinction of analytic and synthetic judgments; and this distinction Kant clearly refers to the Leibnizian distinction between the principles of contradiction and of sufficient reason, or of identity and differentiation. It is not meant that Kant came to this thought through the definitions of Leibniz; on the contrary, Kant himself refers it to Hume's distinction between matters of fact and relations of ideas. But when Kant had once generalized the thought of Hume, it fell at once, as into ready prepared moulds, into the categories of Leibniz. He never escapes from the Leibnizian distinction. In his working of it out consists his greatness as the founder of modern thought; from his acceptance of it as ultimate result his contradictions. That is to say, Kant did not merely receive the vague idea of sufficient reason: he so connected it with what he learned from Hume that he transformed it into the idea of synthesis, and proceeded to work out the conception of synthesis in the various notions of the understanding, or categories, as applicable to the material of sense. What Leibniz bequeathed him was the undefined idea that knowledge of matters of fact rests upon the principle of sufficient reason. What Kant did with this inheritance was to identify the wholly vague idea of sufficient reason with the notion that every fact of experience rests upon necessary synthetic connection, — that is, connection according to notions of understanding with other facts, — and to determine, so far as he could, the various forms of synthesis, or of sufficient reason. With Leibniz the principle remained essentially infertile, because it was the mere notion of the ultimate reference of experience to understanding. In the hands of Kant it became the instrument of revolutionizing philosophy, because Kant showed the articulate members of understanding by which experience is constituted, and described them in the act of constituting.

So much for his working out of the thought. But on the other hand, Kant never transcended the absoluteness of the distinction between the principles of synthesis and analysis, of sufficient reason and contradiction. The result was that he regarded the synthetic principle as the principle only of our knowledge, while perfect knowledge he still considered to follow the law of identity, of mere analysis. He worked out the factor of negation, of differentiation, contained in the notion of synthesis, but limited it to synthesis upon material of sense, presupposing that there is another kind of knowledge, not limited to sense, not depending upon the synthetic principle, but resting upon the principle of contradiction, or analysis, and that this kind is the type, the norm, of the only perfect knowledge. In other words, while admitting the synthetic principle of differentiation as a necessary element within *our* knowledge, he held that on account of this element our knowledge is limited to the phenomenal realm. Leibniz's error was in supposing that the pure principles of the logical understanding, resting on contradiction, could give *us* knowledge of the noumenal world; his truth was in supposing that only by such principles *could* they be known. Thus, in substance, Kant. Like Leibniz, in short, he failed to transcend the absoluteness of the value of the scholastic method; but he so worked out another and synthetic method, — the *development* of the idea of sufficient reason, — that he made it necessary for his successors to transcend it.

The second point concerns the relations of the sensuous and the super-sensuous. Here, besides setting right the ordinary misconception of Leibniz, Kant did nothing but render him consistent with himself. Leibniz attempted to prove the existence of God, as we have seen, by the principles both of sufficient reason and contradiction. Kant denies the validity of the proof by either method. God is the sufficient cause, or reason, of the contingent sense world. But since Leibniz admits that this contingent world may, after all, be but a dream, how shall we rise from it to the notion of God? It is not our dreams that demonstrate to us the existence of reality. Or, again, sense-knowledge is confused knowledge. How shall this knowledge, by hypothesis imperfect, guarantee to us the existence of a perfect being? On the other hand, since the synthetic principle, or that of sufficient reason, *is* necessary to give us knowledge of matters of fact, the principle of contradiction, while it may give us a consistent and even necessary notion of a supreme being, cannot give this notion reality. Leibniz, while admitting, with regard to all other matters of fact, that the principles of formal logic can give no unconditional knowledge, yet supposes that, with regard to the one unconditional reality, they are amply sufficient. Kant but renders him self-consistent on this point.

It is, however, with regard to the doctrine of pre-established harmony that Kant's large measure of indebtedness to Leibniz is most apt to be overlooked. Kant's claim that Leibniz himself meant the doctrine in a subjective sense (that is, of a harmony between powers in our own intelligence) rather than objective (or between things out of relation to intelligence) seems, at first sight, to go far beyond the mark. However, when we recall that to Leibniz the sense world is only the confused side of rational thought, there is more truth in Kant's saying than appears at this first sight. The harmony is between sense and reason. But it may at least be said without qualification that Kant only translated into subjective terms, terms of intelligence, what appears in Leibniz as objective. This is not the place to go into the details of Kant's conception of the relation of the material to the psychical, of the body and the soul. We may state, however, in his own words, that "the question is no longer as to the possibility of the association of the soul with other known and foreign substances outside it, but as to the connection of the presentations of inner sense with the modifications of our external sensibility." It is a question, in short, of the harmony of two modes of our own presentation, not of the harmony of two independent things. And Kant not only thus deals with the fact of harmony, but he admits, as its *possible* source, just what Leibniz claims to be its *actual* source; namely, some one underlying reality, which Leibniz calls the monad, but to which Kant gives no name. "I can well suppose," says Kant, "that the substance to which through external sense extension is attributed, is also the subject of the presentations given to us by its inner sense: *thus that which in one respect is called material being would be in another respect thinking being.*"

Kant treats similarly the problem of the relations of physical and final causes, of necessity and freedom. Here, as in the case just mentioned, his main problem is to discover their *harmony*. His solution, again, is in the union, in our intelligence, of the understanding — as the source of the notions which "make nature" — with the ideas of that reason which gives a "categorical imperative." The cause of the possibility of this harmony between nature and freedom, between the sense world and the rational, he finds in a being, God, whose sole function in the Kantian philosophy may be said to be to "pre-establish" it. I cannot believe that Kant, in postulating the problems of philosophy as the harmony of sense and understanding, of nature and freedom, and in finding this harmony where he did, was not profoundly influenced, consciously as well as unconsciously, by Leibniz. In fact, I do not think that we can understand the nature either of Kant's immense contributions to modern thought or of his inconsistencies, until we have traced them to their source in the Leibnizian philosophy, — admitting, on the other hand, that we cannot understand why Kant should have found necessary a new way of approach to the results of Leibniz, until we recognize to the full his indebtedness to Hume. It was, indeed, Hume that awoke him to his endeavors, but it was Leibniz who set before him the goal of these endeavors. That the goal should appear somewhat transformed, when approached from a new point of view, was to be expected. But alas! the challenge from Hume did not wholly awaken Kant. He still accepted without question the validity of the scholastic method,— the analytic principle of identity as the type of perfect knowledge,— although denying its sufficiency for human intelligence. Leibniz suggested, and suggested richly, the synthetic, the negative aspect of thought; Kant worked it out as a necessary law of *our* knowledge; it was left to his successors to work it out as a factor in the law of *all* knowledge.

It would be a grievous blunder to suppose that this final chapter annihilates the earlier ones; that the failure of Leibniz as to method, though a failure in a fundamental point, cancelled his splendid achievements. Such thoughts as that substance is activity; that its process is measured by its end, its idea; that the universe is an inter-related unit; the thoughts of organism, of continuity, of uniformity of law, — introduced and treated as Leibniz treated them, — are imperishable. They are members of the growing consciousness, on the part of intelligence, of its own nature. There are but three or four names in the history of thought which can be placed by the side of Leibniz's in respect to the open largeness, the unexhausted fertility, of such thoughts. But it is not enough for intelligence to have great thoughts nor even true thoughts. It is testimony to the sincerity and earnestness of intelligence that it cannot take even such thoughts as those of Leibniz on trust. It must *know* them; it must have a method adequate to their demonstration. And in a broad sense, the work of Kant and of his successors was the discovery of a method which should justify the objective idealism of Leibniz, and which in its history has more than fulfilled this task.